M000236747

QUICK QUILT PROJECTS

with Jelly Rolls, Fat Quarters, Honeybuns and Layer Cakes

by Darlene Zimmerman

quick QUILT PROJECTS

with Jelly Rolls, Fat Quarters, Honeybuns *and* Layer Cakes

by Darlene Zimmerman

KP CRAFT
Cincinnati, Ohio

Table of Contents

Introduction

Those tempting morsels—the yummy jelly rolls, honeybuns, layer cakes—who can resist?

We bring those delicious morsels of fabric home,
but then we don't know what recipe to use to make a
tempting treat. Let this book inspire you with a variety
of projects from quick and easy pincushions to snuggly
quilts in a rainbow of colors and flavors.

Using pre-cuts will allow you to "taste test" new
collections and provide a wide variety of fabrics for very
little dough. Whip up your favorite patterns in a range
of colors and sizes.

Every effort is made to use the latest fabrics available,
but if you can no longer find the collections listed in the
"recipes," feel free to let your imagination soar. Use any
bundle of fabric you've already collected, the leftover
scraps from another project, or a new pre-cut bundle
that inspires you to create your masterpiece.

CHAPTER ONE
small projects

New to quilting? More comfortable with crafting than quilting? Try some of these small projects when you have a few minutes to spare. Using pre-cut fabrics such as jelly rolls, charm packs and layer cakes can save time in the cutting process, and you won't need to purchase yards of fabric. Just a taste is all that's needed for these small projects!

No sewing machine? No problem. Many of these small projects can be sewn by hand. Not much time? Again, small projects are the answer. They are something you can complete in a short amount of time with limited resources.

Encourage yourself to work with a new shape, try a new technique and create something beautiful and functional! Choose your own color palette and trims to make the project your own.

FLOWER POWER

Add a delightful surprise to a tote, hat, purse or pillow with some of these colorful posies. Make one, two or three different sizes and stack them up or use them singly. Show your creative side to the world!

Materials

- One layer cake (I used *Ticklish* by Moda)
- Thin polyester batting
- Hand quilting or sewing-weight thread

Tools

- Template plastic or freezer paper
- Traceable *Flower* and *Yo-Yo* templates provided
- Needle

FINISHED DIMENSIONS

5", 7" and 9" (12.5cm, 18cm and 23cm) flowers

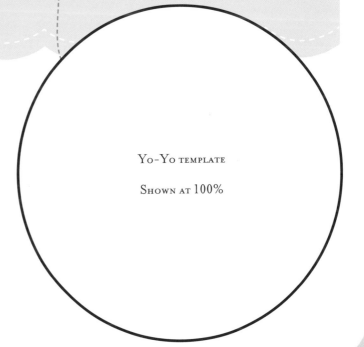

Yo-Yo template

Shown at 100%

Making the Stacked Flowers

1 Make a template of each of the different size flowers using the patterns provided at the end of this project and some template plastic or freezer paper. Use these templates to trace each of the flowers onto the right side of the fabric (folded in half, then half again) chosen for the flower (the fabric should be at least 10", 8" or 6" (25cm, 20.5cm or 15cm) square depending on the size of the flower you're cutting). Cut on the lines. (*Figure 1*)

2 Cut a 10", 8" and 6" (22.5cm, 20.5cm and 15cm) square of fabric for the back of each flower. Cut the same size squares of the batting.

3 Layer the batting and the backing square right side up, and the cutout flower wrong side up. Pin them together, then sew a scant ¼" (6mm) seam just inside the outer edge of the flower. Repeat for each of the flowers. (*Figure 2*)

4 Trim away all the layers to a scant ¼" (6mm) seam allowance. Clip at the inner points and notch the curves if necessary.

5 Cut a 1½" (3.8cm) slit in the top layer of the flower; turn the flower through the opening. Use a blunt tool to open each of the petals. Lightly steam press the flowers. Sew the opening closed.

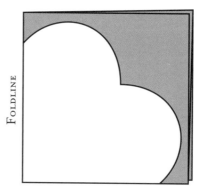

FIGURE 1

FOLD THE FABRIC TWICE, RIGHT SIDE UP, AND CUT ALONG THE LINE OF THE FLOWER TEMPLATE.

FIGURE 2

BATTING AND BACKING RIGHT SIDE UP WITH FLOWER FABRIC WRONG SIDE UP. STITCH ¼" (6MM) INSIDE THE FLOWER.

Making the Yo-Yos

1 Trace and create a template for the yo-yo circle. Trace the circle onto the fabric chosen for the center yo-yo. Cut it out on the line.

2 To make the yo-yo, take a 20" (51cm) length of hand-quilting thread (or a doubled strand of sewing-weight thread), and sew a running stitch around the edge of the circle, turning it under ¼" (6mm) as you stitch. The stitches should be ⅜" (1cm) long and have ⅜" (1cm) between the stitches. When you have stitched completely around the circle, pull the thread to gather tightly and knot the ends.

Assembling the Stacked Flowers

1 Layer the largest flower on the bottom, then the medium size flower, with the smallest flower on top.

2 Sew the yo-yo to the center of the flower stack, through all the layers and in the middle of the yo-yo. Also slipstitch around the edges of the yo-yo, attaching it to the top flower.

3 Sew or pin the stacked flowers to a finished tote, hat, purse or pillow.

FLOWER TEMPLATES

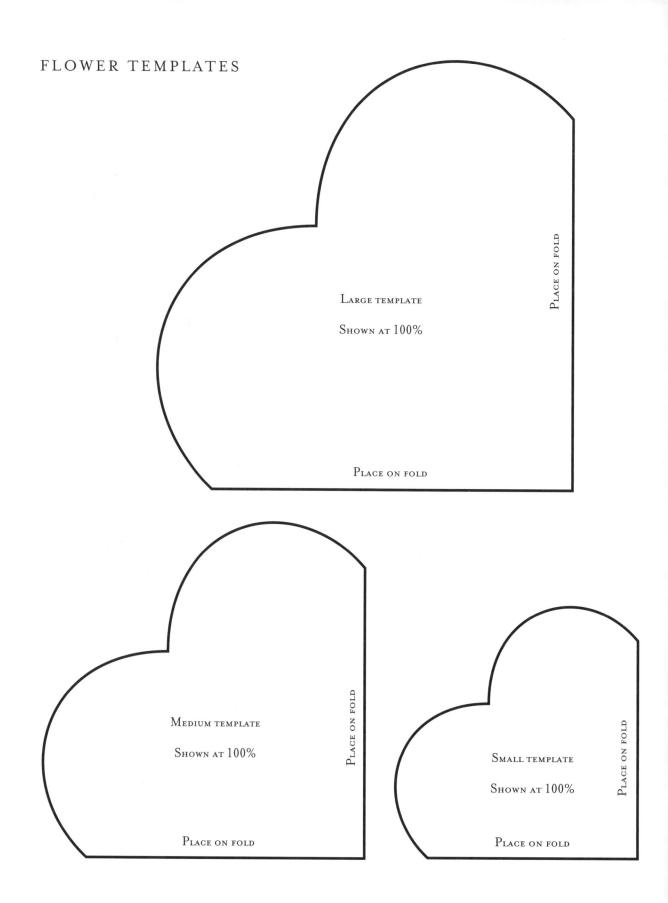

Large template

Shown at 100%

Place on fold

Place on fold

Medium template

Shown at 100%

Place on fold

Place on fold

Small template

Shown at 100%

Place on fold

Place on fold

FLOWER SCARF

Yo-yos make up this cheerful scarf so you can enjoy wearing your spring flowers. The flowers are fun to make and are a great take-along or travel project. Choose flower colors to match a favorite outfit or mix and match colors like Mother Nature does.

Materials

- I dessert roll or ten 5" × 42" (12.5cm 106.5cm) strips (I used Darlene Zimmerman's '30s Reproduction Fabrics by Robert Kaufman Co.)
- Hand-quilting or sewing-weight thread

Tools

- EZ Large Yo-Yo's (EZ Quilting no. 882506) or traceable template provided
- Needle

Cutting Directions

Using the template provided, mark 6 circles on each of 8 different colored prints for a total of 48 circles. Cut out on the marked lines.

Using the same template, mark 8 circles on yellow (or contrasting) fabric for flower centers. Cut out on the marked lines.

Using the same template, mark and cut out 13 circles from green fabric for connectors between the flowers.

FINISHED DIMENSIONS
$4\frac{1}{2}$" × 44" (11.5cm × 112cm)

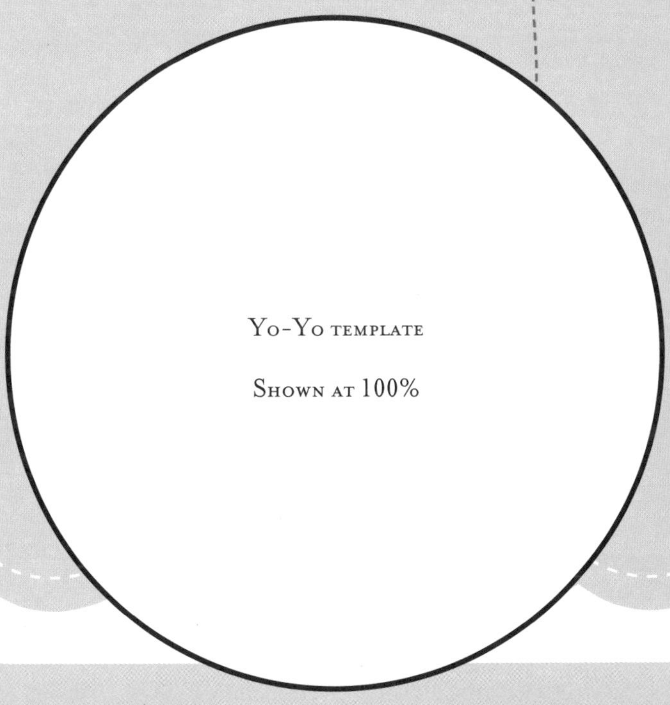

Yo-Yo TEMPLATE

SHOWN AT 100%

Assembling the Flowers

1 Using 20" (50.8m) single strand of hand-quilting thread (or a double strand of sewing-weight thread), tie a knot on one end. Stitch ⅜" (1cm) running stitches around the circle, turning the edge under ¼" (6mm) as you stitch. (*Figure 1*)

2 After stitching completely around the circle, pull the thread to gather as tightly as possible (no need to completely close the circle). The gathers should be in the center of the yo-yo. Knot the thread. (*Figure 2*) Repeat for each of the yo-yo circles.

3 Starting with a yellow center yo-yo, attach the 6 matching yo-yos around the center by sewing a few overhand stitches where the circles touch each other. (*Figure 3*) Make 8 flowers.

4 Use 2 green yo-yos between each of the flowers making one long row. (Except in the center use only one green yo-yo as shown to make the curve for the neckline.) (*Figure 4*) Your scarf is now finished.

FIGURE 1

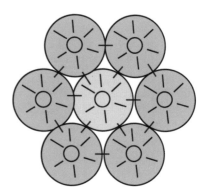

FIGURE 2

FIGURE 3

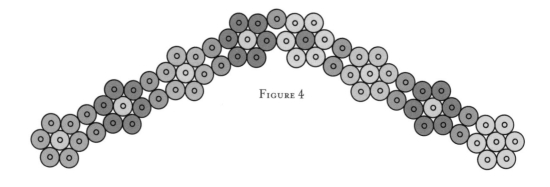

FIGURE 4

HEXAGON PILLOW OR PINCUSHION

A new pillow or two can brighten a room, change the décor from one season to another and add a personal touch to your furniture. Make these adorable pillows in your choice of colors and fabrics to fit with or change your décor. Or, if you prefer, make a special pincushion for yourself or as a gift.

Materials

- 1 jelly roll (I used *Field Notes* by Moda)
- 12" (30.5cm) square for pillow back; 8" (20.5cm) square for pincushion back
- Optional: 12" (30.5cm) square muslin backing and thin batting for each pillow; 8" (20.5cm) square of muslin and thin batting for pincushion
- Polyfil
- Thread

Tools

- Hexagon template sheet (EZ Quilting no. 882505), Mini hexagon tool (EZ Quilting no. 882191) or traceable template provided
- Large Yo-Yo's template (EZ Quilting no. 882506) or traceable template provided
- Needle

FINISHED DIMENSIONS
Large 9" × 10" (23cm × 25.5cm)
Small 6" × 7" (15cm × 18cm)

Cutting Directions

HOW TO CUT HEXAGONS

For each pillow choose 4 coordinating fabrics:
Center: Cut 1 hexagon (A)
Inner Ring of Flower: Cut 6 hexagons (B)
Outer Ring of Flower: Cut 12 hexagons (C)
Edge of Flower: Cut 18 half hexagons

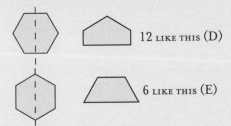

12 LIKE THIS (D)

6 LIKE THIS (E)

Yo-Yo Center: One 2½" (6.5cm) circle for yo-yo

For each pincushion:
Center: cut 1 hexagon
Flower: cut 6 hexagons
Edge of Flower: cut 12 half hexagons

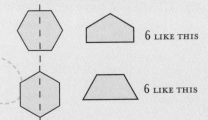

6 LIKE THIS

6 LIKE THIS

Yo-Yo Center: One 2½" (6.5cm) circle for yo-yo

Tip: These projects can be hand-pieced and quilted, which makes them great travel and take-along projects. You can even piece them in the car (if you are not driving).

Assembling the Pillow

NOTE: Because of the small pieces and the inset seams, you may find it easiest to hand-sew the hexagon flower. Before sewing, mark the seam allowances on the wrong side of the hexagons to give yourself a stitching line. Because the pencil mark adds a bit more to the seam allowance, stitch inside (closer to the raw edge) of the marked line. Use a single strand of hand-quilting thread and a running stitch with stitches about ⅛" (3mm) long and ⅛" (3mm) apart. Put several stitches on your needle before pulling it through. Make a small backstitch when you begin again. Backstitch at the seam intersections. Stitch only from seam allowance to seam allowance, not edge to edge as is normally done.

1. With right sides together, join the center hexagon (A) with a hexagon from the first ring (B) along one edge. Pivot at the corner of the seam allowance and sew one more inner ring hexagon to the center piece along two edges. Knot the thread. Repeat to make a complete ring around the center. (*Figures 1 and 2*)

2. In the same manner, join the hexagons for the outer ring (C) of the flower. (*Figures 3 and 4*)

3. Using the half-hexagons (D and E), sew around the edge of the pillow. Pay close attention to the placement of the different shaped half-hexagons. (*Figure 5*)

4. Trim the edges straight using a rotary cutter and ruler. (*Figure 6*)

DRAW A STITCHING LINE AND SEW FROM SEAM ALLOWANCE TO SEAM ALLOWANCE (NOT FROM EDGE TO EDGE).

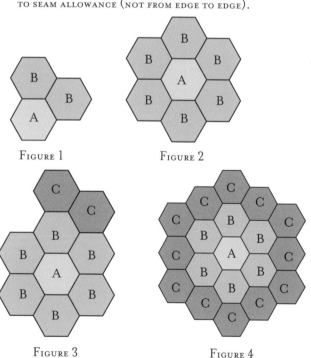

FIGURE 1

FIGURE 2

FIGURE 3

FIGURE 4

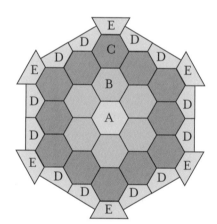

FIGURE 5

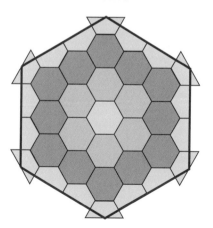

FIGURE 6

Finishing the Pillow (or Pincushion)

1 Optional: Layer the muslin, the thin batting and the hexagon flower top. Baste, then quilt as desired. The projects shown were hand-quilted ¼" (6mm) from the edge of the seams.

2 Baste around the edge of the flower to hold the layers together and prevent shifting.

3 Layer the flower and the backing square right sides together. Stitch around the edges of the flower with a ¼" (6mm) seam, leaving a 2" to 3" (5cm to 7.5cm) opening along one side. Turn right side out.

4 Stuff the flower pillow and sew the opening closed by hand.

5 Using the 2½" (6.5cm) contrasting yo-yo circle and a 20" (51cm) length of thread doubled, stitch ⅜" (1cm) stitches around the edge of the circle, turning the edge under ¼" (6mm) as you stitch. (*Figure 1*) Pull to gather and create the yo-yo. (*Figure 2*) Sew the yo-yo to the center of the pillow, sewing through all the layers and pulling it tightly. Stitch through several times, then knot. Your pillow or pincushion is now ready to use and enjoy!

1

2

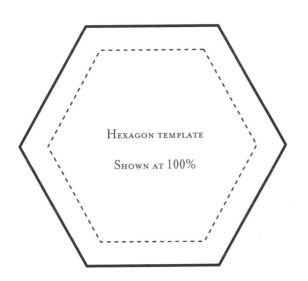

HEXAGON TEMPLATE

SHOWN AT 100%

YO-YO TEMPLATE

SHOWN AT 100%

POTTERY PINCUSHIONS

Colorful pottery planters originating in the '30s, which feature animals, people or household items, can make darling pincushions for yourself or friends! You can also find a new teacup, bowl or candleholder (thrift shops are a great place to look) that will serve the purpose. For best results, look for a container with a fairly small opening, or with an opening that has a tighter rim around it to hold the pincushion in place. In a few minutes, you can transform these everyday items into adorable yet practical pincushions.

Materials

- Planter, teacup or candle holder
- 5"–7" (12.5cm–18cm) square of fabric (depending upon the size of the opening)
- Stuffing
- Hand-quilting thread

Tools

- Needle

Pincushion Assembly

The size of the opening varies with planters, but for most a 6" (15cm) square of fabric is sufficient.

1 Stitch a circle of long gathering stitches (longer stitches) on the 6" (15cm) square using double thread for strength. Pull the threads to make a small pouch. (Figure 1)

2 Stuff with polyester or wool (remnants of batting can be pulled apart and used for this purpose). Stuff tightly, then pull the gathering thread tight and fasten off. (Figure 2)

3 Use more batting or stuffing to fill up the base of the planter before inserting the pincushion. If you wish to weight the planter, add pebbles, rice or sand. Filling the planter base will prevent the pincushion from being pushed down into the planter.

4 Insert the pincushion so it fits snugly into the opening (no need for hot glue!). Add some colorful pins to complete the look and you have instant gifts or décor!

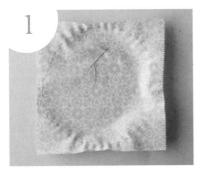

WOVEN PLACE MATS

Easy-to-make yet charming, these place mats can be used as a gift for yourself or for others. They are fast to make, since the jelly roll strips are pre-cut and you quilt the place mats as you assemble them. Choose fabrics that coordinate with your dishes and décor. If you use all the strips, one jelly roll could make a dozen place mats!

Materials

- 1 jelly roll (I used the *Fusions Ombre* collection from Robert Kaufman)
- **Backing and Binding:** 1½ yds. (1.4m)
- **Cotton Batting:** 4 rectangles exactly 14" × 19" (35.5cm × 48.5cm)

Tools

- Blue water-soluble pen
- Walking foot for your sewing machine

Cutting Directions

Backing: Cut four 14½" × 19" (35.5cm × 48.5cm) rectangles. Cut the remaining fabric into seven 2¼" × 42" (5.5cm × 106.5cm) straight-of-grain strips for binding.

Jelly roll: For 4 place mats, cut 14 strips into three 2½" × 14" (6.5cm × 35.5cm) rectangles (or after trimming selvages, divide them into 3 equal sections) for a total of 42 rectangles.

FINISHED DIMENSIONS
4 place mats at 13½" × 18½" (34.5cm × 47cm)

Assembling the Place Mats

1 Place the backing wrong side up, then place the batting rectangle on top, matching the raw edges. Mark several vertical lines on the batting with a blue water-soluble pen to keep the strips straight while sewing. Place the first strip, right side up, on the left-hand side, aligned with the left edge of the batting and backing. Using the walking foot, baste a scant ¼" (6mm) from the left edge of the place mat through all the layers. (*Figure 1*)

2 Lay a second strip on top of the first strip, right sides together, and sew a ¼" (6mm) seam through all the layers, using the walking foot to prevent shifting. Open out the second strip and finger press the seam to one side. Repeat, sewing a total of 10 strips and keeping the strips aligned with the vertical lines marked on the batting. Make a total of 4 place mats. (*Figures 2 and 3*) You will have two strips left over.

3 From the back side of the place mat, trim the edges evenly to 13½" × 18½" (34.5cm × 47cm) or make sure all of the place mats are the same size. Baste a scant ¼" (6mm) around the edge to hold the layers together for binding. (See *General Instructions* for more information on binding.)

Finishing the Place Mats

Prepare the binding strips by joining with diagonal seams pressed open. Fold in half the long way and press to make a double binding. Sew to the place mats with a ¼" (6mm) seam, mitering the corners. (See *General Instructions* for more information on mitered corners.)

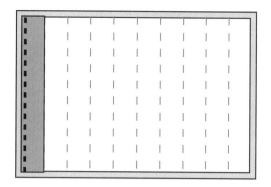

FIGURE 1

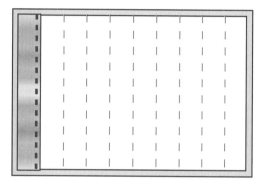

FIGURE 2

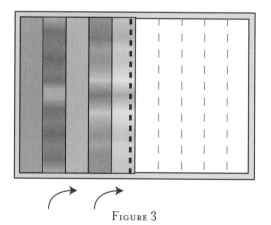

FIGURE 3

DAISY PATCH VALANCE

The original name of this pattern is *Joseph's Coat*. It is an old quilt pattern that was quite challenging to make. I've used an updated (and much easier) version of the pattern to create a lovely scalloped-edge window valance. I've renamed the pattern *Daisy Patch* as it reminds me of the flower.

Materials

- **White background**: 1¼ yds. (1.1m)
- **Variety of prints**: 1 jelly roll
- **Yellow solid**: ¼ yd. (23cm) or fat quarter
- **Binding**: Fat quarter
- **Backing and sleeve**: 1½ yds. (1.4m)
- **Batting**: 30" × 52" (76cm × 132cm)
- Thread

Tools

- *Joseph's Coat* template set (EZ Quilting no. 882503) or traceable templates provided
- Optional: Freezer paper, liquid starch, small paintbrush
- Needle

Cutting Directions

From white, cut seven 5½" × 42" (14cm × 106.5cm) strips. From those strips cut a total of 56 triangle shapes. (A)

From the jelly roll strips, cut a total of 87 petal shapes. (B)

From the yellow solid, cut a total of 36 circles. (C)

FINISHED DIMENSIONS
23½" × 47½" (60cm × 121cm)

To fit your window, decide upon the length and width you need, and adjust the number of pieces you need to cut.

Tip: To make it easier to appliqué the circles, cut 2 smaller circles (without the seam allowance) from freezer paper. Fuse the 2 circles together (shiny side to dull side) to make a double thick circle and iron it to the wrong side of the solid yellow fabric. Cut out, adding a ¼" (6mm) seam allowance. Using liquid starch and a small paintbrush, wet the seam allowance of the fabric circles and iron over the edge of the freezer paper circles. The edges will be turned under nicely, and the freezer paper templates can be removed and used again.

Assembling the Valance

1 Sew a white triangle shape on top of a petal shape, matching the flat ends and easing the curved edge while sewing. Finger press toward the petal shape. *(Figure 1)*

2 Continue sewing petals and triangle shapes together following the diagram below. *(Figure 2)*

3 Appliqué or fuse the yellow circles in place over the openings in each flower, even on the edges of the valance (as shown in the diagram). See the tip at the beginning of the pattern for more information on preparing the circles.

4 Based on measurements taken of the window, sew petals and triangles until the valance has the correct dimensions. Trim the upper edge of the valance straight across. *(Figure 3)*

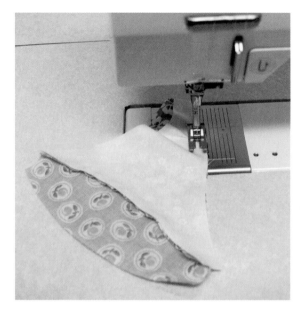

FIGURE 1

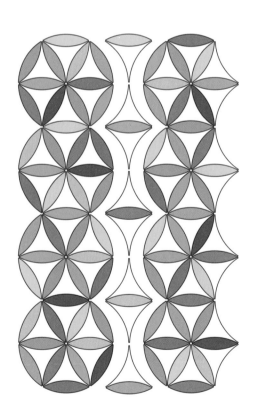

FIGURE 2

FIGURE 3

Finishing the Valance

1 Trim the batting and backing several inches larger than the valance top all the way around.

2 Sew the trimmed top edge of the valance, right sides together, with the backing. Turn and press. Tuck the batting between the layers, right up to the seam. Baste the layers together.

3 Quilt as desired. Before binding, baste the raw edges of the valance together a scant ¼" (6mm) from the edges to prevent the layers from shifting.

4 Cut 1¼"-wide (3.2mm-wide) single bias binding strips from the fat quarter. Join with diagonal seams; press open. Sew the binding to the quilt with a ¼" (6mm) seam, pivoting in the inner yellow circles and smoothing out the curve on the outer yellow circles. (See *General Instructions* for more instruction on binding curved edges.)

5 Trim the excess batting, backing and quilt top edges to an even ¼" (6mm) seam allowance. Turn the binding to the back side, turn under ¼" (6mm), and stitch down by hand with matching thread.

6 Cut a 5" (12.5cm) wide by the length of the valance strip from the remaining backing fabric. Fold it under ¼" (6mm) and stitch it on all sides. Hand-baste the sleeve to the top edge of the back of the valance. Insert a curtain rod of your choice and hang.

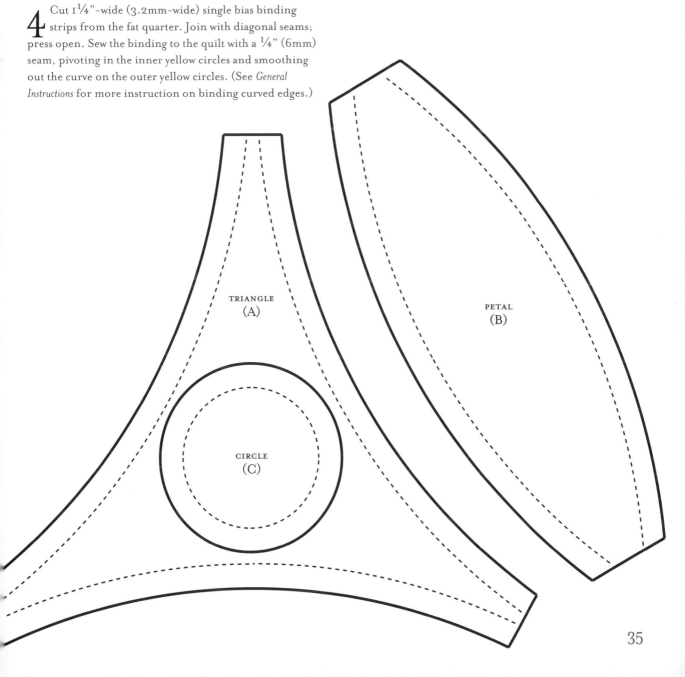

TRIANGLE
(A)

CIRCLE
(C)

PETAL
(B)

THE MANLY FOOTSTOOL

Discover the comfort of the old-fashioned footstool. It's a wonderful feeling at the end of the day to sit down, put your feet up, and relax with your favorite beverage and a good book. Order a footstool kit or recover a footstool that you find at a thrift store or garage sale (or build your own if you're handy). Make this Manly Footstool for yourself or that special person in your life.

Materials

- One footstool to cover (Simplicity kit no. 1475119030). Remove the legs if possible.
- 1 jelly roll (I used *Woolies Flannel* from Maywood Studios) or pack of charm squares

Tools

- Heavy-duty staple gun, tacks or duct tape
- 60° diamond template (EZ Quilting no. 882670182A, mini template no. 882187 or traceable template provided)

Cutting Directions

Using the diamond template, cut a total of 56 diamonds from the jelly roll strips.

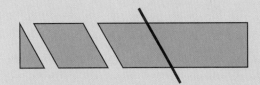

FINISHED DIMENSIONS

Footstool top is 17" × 12" (43cm × 30cm)

If using a different size footstool, adjust the length and width of the top to fit. The cover should wrap around the footstool with enough extra fabric to fasten to the bottom.

60° DIAMOND TEMPLATE

SHOWN AT 100%

Assembling the Footstool

1 Mark a ¼" (6mm) seam allowance on 1 diagonal edge of a diamond. Position the diamond, right sides together, on top of another diamond. Use the marked ¼" (6mm) seam line to align the diamonds accurately as shown. Stitch. (*Figure 1*)

2 Sew 8 diamonds together in a row. Press the seams open. Repeat to make 4 more rows aligned the same direction. (*Figure 2*)

3 In the same manner, sew 8 diamonds together facing the opposite direction. Press the seams open. Make 3 more rows this way. (*Figure 3*)

4 Sew the step 2 and step 3 rows together, matching seams, to make the footstool cover. Press the seams open. (*Figure 4*)

5 Square the jagged ends of the cover. If needed, sew a narrow strip of fabric to each of the long ends to make it long enough to fasten underneath. (*Figure 4*)

6 Turn the cover under ¼" (6mm) along all edges. Pull the footstool cover over the top and fasten down one long edge with staples, tacks or duct tape. On the opposite side, pull the fabric taut, making sure to keep the stripes straight, and fasten down. (*Figure 5*)

7 Repeat the same procedure for the short ends of the footstool cover, folding in the corners neatly. If need be, trim any excess fabric that may show. (*Figure 6*)

8 Attach the legs (unless they haven't been removed) to the stool and put your feet up!

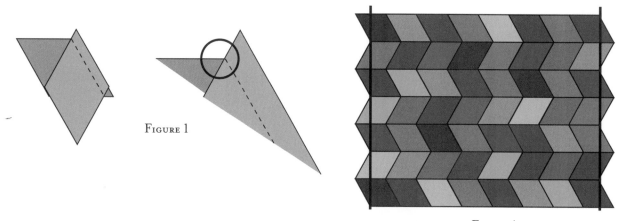

FIGURE 1

FIGURE 4

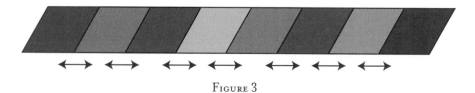

FIGURE 2

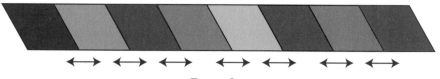

FIGURE 3

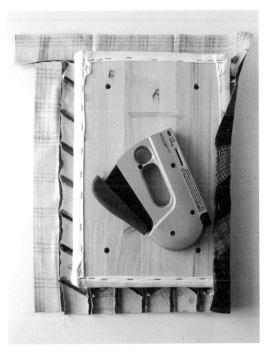

FIGURE 5

FIGURE 6

SWEET AND SIMPLE TABLE RUNNER

After making the *Summertime Quilt* (see Chapter Two), I found I had plenty of red jelly roll strips leftover. This table runner was designed to use some of those leftover strips, but any leftover fabric from jelly rolls or other projects will work—you only need to have lights and darks.

Beginning quilters are often afraid to sew triangles. Don't be! Many quilt patterns use triangles, so don't limit yourself to only squares and rectangles. You'll have plenty of practice sewing triangles on this small table runner. This project is simple to make and easy to machine- or hand-quilt. Give it a try!

For the pastel version, I used jelly roll strips from *Pearl Essence* by Galaxy for E.E. Schenck Co.

Materials

- 4 red jelly roll strips for triangles
- **Border:** 3 red jelly roll strips of 1 print for borders (or ¼ yd. [23cm])
- 4 white jelly roll strips for triangles (or ⅓ yd. [30cm] cut into four 2½" × 42" [6.5cm × 106.5cm] strips)
- **Backing:** ⅝ yd. (57.2cm)
- **Binding:** 3 matching red jelly roll strips (or ¼ yd. [23cm]), trimmed to 2¼" (5.5cm) wide
- **Batting:** 18" × 36" (46cm × 91.5cm)

Tools

- EZ Angle (EZ Quilting no. 8823759A), Mini EZ Angle (EZ Quilting no. 882188) or traceable template provided
- Needle

FINISHED DIMENSIONS
16" × 32" (40.5cm × 81.5cm)
4" (10cm) blocks

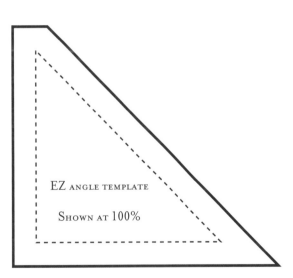

EZ ANGLE TEMPLATE

SHOWN AT 100%

Assembling the Table Runner

NOTE: If your jelly roll strips are slightly wider than 2½" (6.5cm), trim off some of the pinked edges so the strips equal exactly 2½"-wide (6.5cm-wide). Most pre-cuts have pinked edges.

1 Layer one red and one white strip right sides together. Repeat with the remaining strips. With the EZ Angle, cut a total of 84 sets of triangles. Sew into triangle-squares. Press toward the red triangle. Trim dog ears. At this point, each triangle-square should measure 2½" (6.5cm). (*Figure 1*)

2 Sew the triangle-squares together in pairs, exactly as shown. Press as shown. (*Figure 2*)

3 Sew the pairs together in blocks, matching and pinning the centers. Twist the seam to open, so the seams all spin around the center. (See *General Instructions* for this technique.) Make 21 blocks. At this point the blocks should measure 4½" (11.5cm) square. (*Figure 3*)

4 Match and pin seam intersections, then sew the blocks together in 3 rows of 7 blocks. Press the seams in the rows in alternating directions. Sew the rows together, matching and pinning seam intersections. Press the long seams open to reduce bulk.

Borders

1 Measure and cut 2 border strips the width of the table runner. Sew to the top and bottom of the table runner. Press the seams toward the borders.

2 Piece the side borders as needed, then measure and cut 2 borders the length of the table runner. Sew to each side and press the seams toward the borders.

Finishing the Quilt

1 Layer the backing wrong side up, the batting, and the quilt top right side up. Baste, then quilt as desired. For easy machine quilting, stitch in the ditch horizontally as well as vertically with a walking foot. Quilt a design in the border.

2 Before binding, hand-baste (or use a walking foot) a scant ¼" (6mm) from the edge of the runner to hold the layers together.

3 Prepare the binding strips by joining with diagonal seams pressed open. Fold in half, wrong sides together and press to make a double binding. Sew to the quilt with a ¼" (6mm) seam, mitering the corners. (See *General Instructions* for more instruction on binding.)

4 Trim excess batting and backing, turn the binding to the back side and stitch down by hand with matching thread.

Figure 1

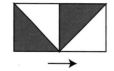

Figure 2

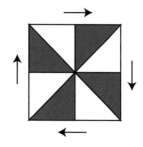

Figure 3

BUTTERFLY GARDEN WALL HANGING

Flowers and butterflies are a pleasing combination on this sweet little wall hanging. Perfect for spring or summer, this quilt will bring a ray of sunshine into your home.

Materials

- 1 pack of charm squares in pastels or '30s prints (at least forty 5" [12.5cm] squares)
- **Light background:** ⅝ yd. (57.2cm)
- **Solid colors:** Scraps
- **Binding:** ⅓ yd. (30.2cm)
- **Batting:** 25" × 35" (63.5cm × 89cm)
- **Backing:** ¾ yd. (68.6cm)
- ½ yd. (45.7cm) fusible web
- 1 skein dark brown or black embroidery floss
- Hand-quilting thread (optional)

Tools

- **EZ Angle** (EZ Quilting no. 8823759A), Mini EZ angle (EZ Quilting no. 882188) or traceable template provided
- *Butterfly* template provided
- Needle

FINISHED DIMENSIONS

22½" × 29" (57cm × 73.5cm)

Cutting Directions

FROM	CUT	TO YIELD
Background	Two 2½" × 42" (6.5cm × 106.5cm) strips	40 Easy Angle triangles
	One 4½" × 42" (11.5cm × 106.5cm) strip	Eight 4½" (11.5cm) squares
	One 2½" × 42" (6.5cm × 106.5cm) strip	Ten 2½" (6.5cm) squares
	Three 1½" × 42" (3.8cm × 106.5cm) strips	Inner borders
Solids	8 coordinating lower wings and 8 bodies	
Charms	8 squares	8 butterfly top wings
	10 squares	Two 2½" × 5" (6.5cm × 12.5cm) rectangles; cut into 4 Easy Angle triangles for pinwheels, total of 40 triangles
	7 squares	Cut each twice diagonally (like an X) to make 28 triangles for setting triangles
	15 squares	Cut each into four 2½" (6.5cm) squares for border
Binding	Three 2¼" × 42" (5.5cm × 106.5cm) strips	Binding strips

Butterfly Blocks

1 Trace 8 upper wings, 8 lower wings and 8 bodies on the paper side of fusible web. Roughly cut out. Fuse each shape to the back of the chosen fabrics. I used a print for the upper wings, a solid color for the lower wings and a brown solid for the bodies. Cut out the fused shapes. (*Figure 1*)

2 Fuse the butterfly wings and bodies on the diagonal of the 4½" (11.5cm) background squares. Make 8 butterfly blocks. Using a small buttonhole stitch and dark brown (or black) thread, stitch around the wings and bodies of the butterflies by hand or machine.

3 Using 2 strands of embroidery floss, embroider the antennae of the butterflies.

Pinwheel Blocks

1 Place a background triangle and a print triangle right sides together. (Be sure to use the Easy Angle triangles with one tip cut off!) Sew on the diagonal. Press to the print triangle. Trim dog-ears. Repeat for each of the print and background triangles. At this point the triangle-squares should measure 2½" (6.5cm) square. Make 40. (*Figure 2*)

2 Sew matching triangle-squares together in pairs. Press as shown. (*Figure 3*)

3 Sew the matching pairs together to make a block. Twist the center seam to pop a few threads; press the seams to spin around the center (see *General Instructions* for this technique). Make 10 blocks. At this point the blocks should measure 4½" (11.5cm). (*Figure 4*)

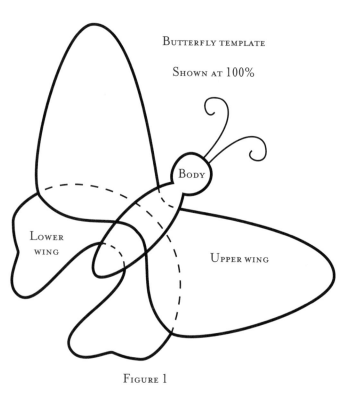

FIGURE 1

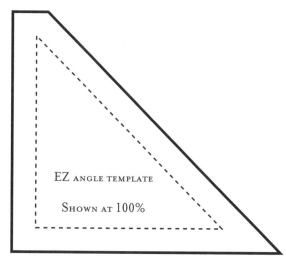

BUTTERFLY TEMPLATE

SHOWN AT 100%

LOWER wing

UPPER WING

Body

EZ ANGLE TEMPLATE

SHOWN AT 100%

FIGURE 2

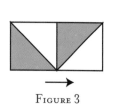

FIGURE 3

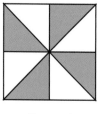

FIGURE 4

Setting Triangles

1 Sew a print triangle to the right side of a background square. Press toward the triangle. Repeat for each of the background squares.

Note: The triangles will be larger than needed. Put the excess at the outer edge. *(Figure 5)*

2 Sew another print triangle to the adjacent side of the square. Press toward the square. Repeat for the remainder of the units. Make 10. *(Figure 6)*

3 For the corner triangles, sew 2 print triangles together. Press as shown. *(Figure 7)* Make 4 corner triangles.

Assembling the Quilt

1 Arrange the setting triangles, the pinwheel blocks and the butterfly blocks in diagonal rows. Sew the blocks and triangles together in rows, pressing each row in alternating directions. *(Figure 8)*

2 Sew the rows together, pinning and matching seam allowances.

3 Trim the outer edges of the quilt straight, leaving a ¼" (6mm) seam allowance from the corners of the background squares.

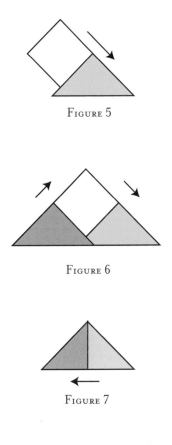

FIGURE 5

FIGURE 6

FIGURE 7

FIGURE 8

Borders

1 Measure and cut 1½" (3.8cm) inner white background borders the width of the quilt. Sew to the top and bottom of the quilt. Press toward the borders. Repeat for the side borders.

2 Sew nine 2½" (6.5cm) print squares together to form the top border. Repeat for the bottom border. Press all seams in one direction. Do not sew to the quilt yet. *(Figure 9)*

3 Sew twelve 2½" (6.5cm) print squares together for the side borders. Press all seams in one direction. (You will use 4 more squares for the corners, and there will be a few squares left over.) *(Figure 10)*

4 Measure the quilt from side to side. Measure the top and bottom borders. Trim the sides of the quilt evenly to the width of the top and bottom pieced borders.

5 Measure the length of the quilt and the side borders. Trim the top and bottom of the quilt evenly to match the length of the side pieced borders. The inner white border does not need to be the same width on the sides as it is on the top and bottom.

6 Sew the top and bottom pieced borders to the quilt top. Press the seams toward the borders added.

7 Sew 2 more 2½" (6.5cm) squares to both of the pieced side borders. Press. Sew the pieced side borders to the sides of the quilt, pressing toward the pieced borders.

Tip: Follow these steps to have the pieced border fit your quilt exactly without tears!

Finishing the Quilt

1 Layer the backing wrong side up with the batting and the quilt top right side up. Baste, then quilt as desired. The quilt shown was stitched in the ditch on all the diagonals of the pinwheels, around the butterflies and on both sides of the background border. The pieced border was also stitched in the ditch. A small meander was quilted in all the background areas.

2 Before binding, hand- or machine-baste a scant ¼" (6mm) from the edge of the quilt with a walking foot.

3 Prepare the binding by joining the binding strips with diagonal seams pressed open. Fold in half, wrong sides together and press to make a double binding. Sew to the quilt with a ¼" (6cm) seam, mitering the corners. (See *General Instructions* for more instructions on binding.)

4 Trim the excess batting and backing; turn the binding to the back side of the quilt and stitch down by hand with matching thread.

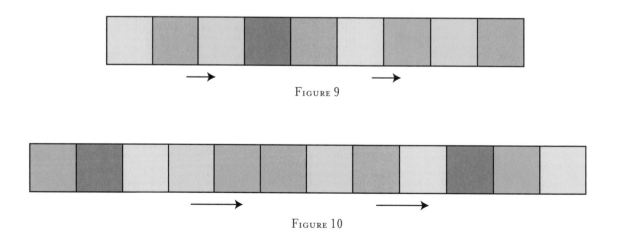

FIGURE 9

FIGURE 10

POT HOLDER BRITCHES

These pot holders are so sweet and so easy to make. Use three coordinating layer cake squares to sew up your cute pot holder britches in no time at all. The pot holders are reversible, so make both sides attractive!

Materials

- 3 coordinating layer cake squares (10" sq. [25.5cm sq.])
- Scraps of cotton batting
- 2 small buttons
- Optional: Narrow 7" (18cm) ribbon for strap

Tools

- Traceable *Britches* templates provided
- Needle

FINISHED DIMENSIONS

9" × 9¾" (23cm × 25cm) at widest and tallest points

Cutting Directions

Fold one of the coordinating squares in half, then cut out one set of britches. Repeat with a second 10" (25.5cm) square.

Cut out 2 britches from the cotton batting using the batting template. **Note:** These are smaller than the fabric ones.

From the last 10" (25.5cm) square, cut the following:

Two 2½" × 8½" (6.5cm × 21.5cm) strips for ruffles

One waistband strip 2¼" × 5" (5.5cm × 12.5cm)

One strap 1¼" × 7" (3.2cm × 18cm). You can also use a ribbon for the strap.

Assembling the Pot Holder

1 Fold the two ruffle strips in half, right sides together, the length of the strips. Sew a ¼" (6mm) seam at both short ends of the 2 strips. Trim the corners, turn and press right sides out. *(Figure 1)*

2 Gather or fold ¼" (6mm) deep pleats the length of the ruffle strip. The ruffle strip needs to measure about 3½" (9cm) in length. Sew the ruffles, raw edges together, on the two legs of one of the britches ¼" inside the side seam allowances. *(Figures 2 and 3)*

3 With right sides together, sew the two britches together, leaving the top waistband area open. Clip the bottom curve between the legs. Turn and press. *(Figures 3 & 4)*

4 Tuck the two layers of batting inside. Stitch a line down the center of the pot holder to hold the batting in place. *(Figure 5)*

5 Gather the two layers of the waist slightly (stitch long stitches, then pull to gather the length of the waistband).

6 Fold and stitch the waistband as in step 1. Turn. Matching the two raw edges of the waistband to the waist of the britches, sew a ¼" (6mm) seam. Clip threads. Turn the folded edge over the seam and cover the stitching line. Hand sew in place.

7 Fold the short ends of the strap in ¼" (6mm). Press. Fold the strip in half the long way, press. Open the fold and press the long edges to the center fold as shown. Press. Refold, then stitch the strap along the double folded edge. Optional: Use a narrow piece of ribbon for the strap. *(Figure 6)*

8 Hand sew the strap to the pot holder. Sew buttons on the opposite side of the pot holder.

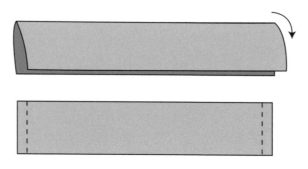

FIGURE 1

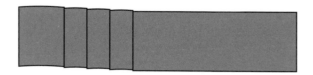

FIGURE 2

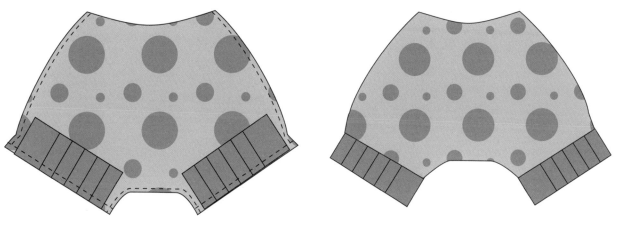

Figure 3

Figure 4

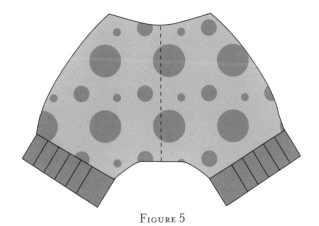

Figure 5

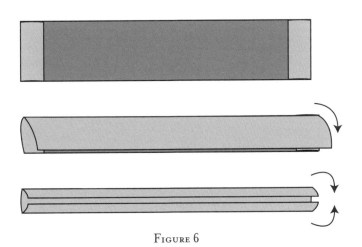

Figure 6

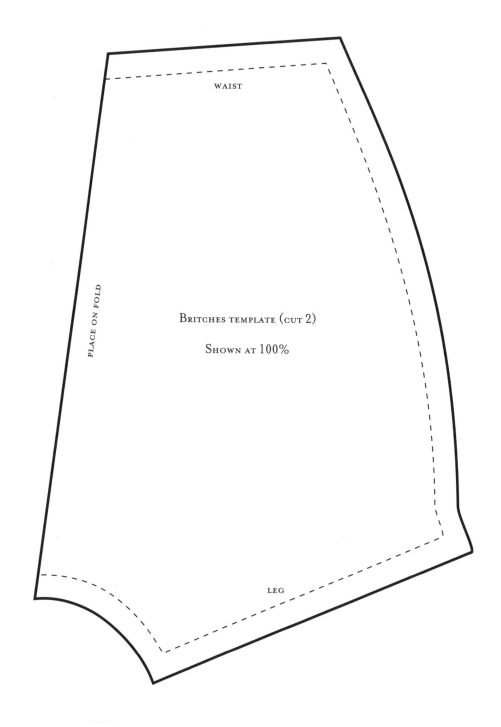

WAIST

PLACE ON FOLD

Britches template (cut 2)

Shown at 100%

LEG

54

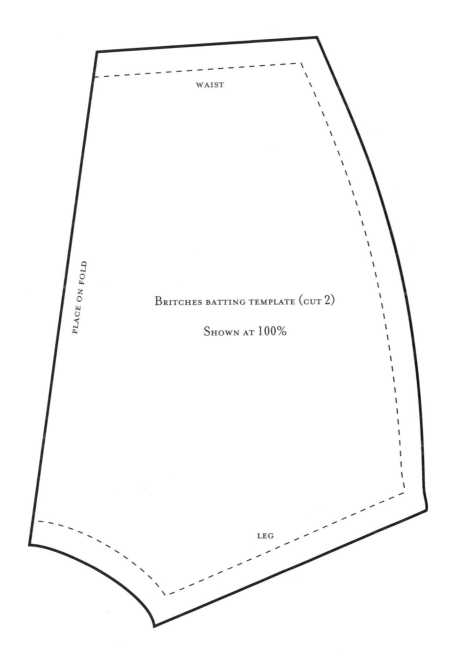

WAIST

PLACE ON FOLD

BRITCHES BATTING TEMPLATE (CUT 2)

SHOWN AT 100%

LEG

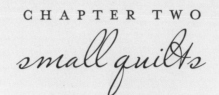

CHAPTER TWO
small quilts

As quilters, we love the whole process of making quilts—choosing fabric, cutting, sewing and of course, finishing a quilt. Admittedly some of the tasks are not as enjoyable as others—cutting is one of those tasks! While the rotary cutter has definitely sped up the cutting process and allows you to cut more accurately, it can still get tedious. That's where the pre-cuts step in to help us out. Not only can you purchase a whole collection in a lovely little package (saving you a bundle of cash), but the pre-cut pieces allow you to quickly move on to the fun part—sewing and creating!

In this chapter, find some great ideas for easy and interesting quilts to make with pre-cut fabrics. Can't find the fabric bundles used for the projects? No worries, just interpret the patterns in your choice of colors.

Or, if you have a large stash to use up, consider making up your own bundles of pre-cuts to use in making the projects in this book. You probably have enough fabric to make up kits for all your quilting friends!

BLUE-AND-WHITE CLASSIC

Shades of indigo-dyed blue cotton fabric have been a favorite choice of quilters for more than a century. The indigo plant has roots that produce a strong, relatively colorfast blue dye. In fact, indigo is still used today to dye our blue jeans!

Quilters have long favored a blue-and-white color scheme; blue-and-white quilts are considered classics. They will work with any color scheme, can look quite modern but also work well with antiques or in a traditional setting, and will never go out of style. Consider making your own blue-and-white classic quilt using this easy pattern and two honeybun rolls.

Materials

- 2 honeybuns with at least 15 light fabrics and 15 dark fabrics per roll (*Indigo Crossing* by Moda was used for the project shown)
- **Block Centers** (blue solid): ¼ yd. (23cm)
- **Border and Binding:** ⅞ yd. (68.6cm)
- **Backing:** 2½ yds. (2.3m)
- **Batting:** Crib size (45" × 60" [114.5cm × 152.5cm])

Tools

- Traceable flower and yo-yo templates provided

FINISHED DIMENSIONS

44" × 52" (112cm × 132cm)
8" (20.5cm) finished blocks

Cutting Directions

From the blue solid for block centers cut:
(30) 2½" (6.5cm) squares

From each of the 30 light fabrics cut:
(2) 1½" × 6½" (3.8cm × 16.5cm) rectangles
(2) 1½" × 4½" (3.8cm × 11cm) rectangles
(2) 1½" × 2½" (3.8cm × 6cm) rectangles

From each of the 30 dark fabrics cut:
(2) 1½" × 8½" (3.8cm × 21.5cm) rectangles
(2) 1½" × 6½" (3.8cm × 16.5cm) rectangles
(2) 1½" × 4½" (3.8cm × 11.5cm) rectangles

From the border and binding fabric cut:
(5) 2½" × 42" (6.5cm × 106.5cm) strips for borders
(5) 2¼" × 42" (5.5cm × 106.5cm) strips for binding

Assembling the Blocks (Make 30)

1 Sew 2 different 1½" × 2½" (3.8cm × 6.5cm) light rectangles to opposite sides of a 2½" (6.5cm) solid blue square. Press toward the light rectangles. *(Figure 1)*

2 Sew 2 different 1½" × 4½" (3.8cm × 11.5cm) dark rectangles to opposite sides of the unite in Figure 1. Press toward the dark rectangles. *(Figure 2)*

3 Sew 1½" × 4½" (3.8cm × 11.5cm) light rectangles to opposite sides of the Figure 2 unit. Press toward the outer edge of the block. *(Figure 3)*

4 Continue sewing light and dark rectangles in the same manner until the block is an 8½" (21.5cm) square. Make 30 blocks. **Note:** Press the last 2 seams on half the blocks towards the center of the block. *(Figures 4 and 5)*

Assembling the Quilt

Alternating the A and B blocks (shown in *Figures 4 and 5*), arrange the blocks into 6 rows of 5 blocks each as shown. *(Figure 6)* Sew the blocks in each row together; press all of the seams in one direction, alternating the direction the seams are pressed in each row. Sew the rows together, pressing the seams open.

Refer to the flat shot of the Blue-and-White Classic quilt on page 110.

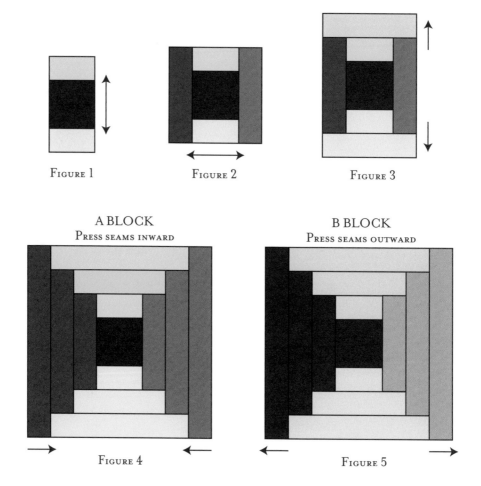

FIGURE 1   FIGURE 2   FIGURE 3

A BLOCK
PRESS SEAMS INWARD

B BLOCK
PRESS SEAMS OUTWARD

FIGURE 4   FIGURE 5

Borders

Measure and cut two 2½" × 42" (6.5cm × 106.5cm) strips the width of the quilt. Sew to the top and bottom of the quilt. Press toward the borders. Piece the remaining side border strips. Measure, cut and sew the side borders to the quilt in the same manner. Press toward the borders.

Finishing the Quilt

1 Trim the batting and backing a few inches larger than the quilt top. Layer the backing wrong side up, the batting and the quilt top right side up. Baste the layers and quilt as desired.

2 Before binding, hand- or machine-baste (using a walking foot) a scant ¼" (6mm) from the edge of the quilt to prevent the layers from shifting while the binding is sewn on.

3 Prepare the 2¼" × 42" (6.5cm × 106.5cm) binding strips by joining with diagonal seams pressed open. Fold the binding in half, wrong sides together and press to make a double binding. Sew to the quilt with a ¼" (6mm) seam allowance, mitering the corners. (See *General Instructions* for more instruction on binding.)

4 Trim the excess batting and backing, turn the binding to the back side and stitch down by hand with matching thread.

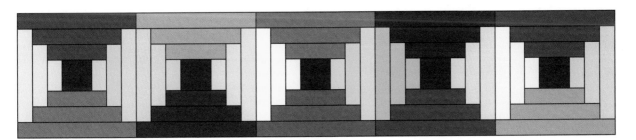

FIGURE 6

CAKEWALK

Traditionally this pattern was called *Brickwalk* because it resembled a brick pavement or wall. However, it was "a piece of cake" to make, so I renamed it *Cakewalk*. What makes it so easy? The pre-cut 5" (12.5cm) charm squares save cutting time, and when you sew the completed rows together there are no seams to match! You'll have fun making this wall hanging or baby quilt with any charm pack.

Materials

- 2 packs of 5" (12.5cm) charm squares with at least 84 charm squares (I used *Lario* by Three Sisters for Moda and *Snap! Pop!* by Sandy Gervais for Moda)
- **Inner Border and Binding:** ¾ yd. (68.6cm)
- **Outer Border:** ⅞ yd. (80cm) for non-directional fabric or 1⅞ yds. (1.7m) for directional fabric
- **Backing:** 2¾ yds. (2.5m)
- **Batting:** Crib size (45" × 60" [114.5cm × 152.5cm])

Tools

- Optional: Easy Scallop (EZ Quilting no. 8823754A)

FINISHED DIMENSIONS
48" × 52" (122cm × 132cm)

Cakewalks were an old-time dancing competition. The prize, of course, was a beautifully decorated cake, but the dancing was done for fun and entertainment. Today we say, "It was a cakewalk," when something was easy and enjoyable to do.

Assembling the Quilt

1 Arrange the charm squares in 10 rows of 8 squares. Sew the squares in each row together, pressing the seams all the same direction. You will have four or more squares left over. *(Figure 1)*

2 Cut each of the rows from step 1 in half lengthwise, making 2 rows that measure 2½" (6.5cm) wide, for a total of 20 rows. *(Figure 2)*

3 Take 10 of the 2½" (6.5cm) wide rows and trim 2¼" (5.5cm) off of one end. *(Figure 3)*

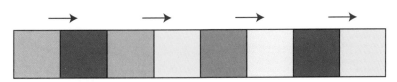

Figure 1

4 Using the remaining 5" (12.5cm) squares, cut each square in half, making 2½" × 5" (6.5cm × 12.5cm) rectangles. Trim the rectangles to 2½" × 2¾" (6.5cm × 7cm). *(Figure 4)* You will need a total of ten 2½" × 2¾" (6.5cm × 7cm) rectangles. (If necessary, use the scraps pieced together or cut a 2½" × 42" [6.5cm × 106.5cm] strip from your outer border fabric to cut the required number of 2½" × 2¾" [6.5cm × 7cm] rectangles.)

5 Sew the rectangles from step 4 to the untrimmed ends of the Figure 3 rows.

6 Alternating the rows beginning with full bricks with the rows beginning with half bricks, arrange in 20 rows. Sew the rows together, pinning so they don't shift while sewing. Press all of the seams in one direction.

Borders

1 For the inner border, cut five 1½" × 42" (3.8cm × 106.5cm) strips. Measure and trim 2 strips the width of the quilt. Sew to the top and bottom of the quilt. Press the seams toward the borders. Piece the remaining 3 strips. Measure and cut 2 borders the length of the quilt. Sew to the sides and press the seams toward the borders.

2 For non-directional fabrics, cut five 5½" × 42" (14cm × 106.5cm) strips from the outer border fabric. For directional fabrics, cut two 5½" × 42" (14cm × 106.5cm) strips for the top and bottom border, and cut two 5½" × 53" (14cm × 134.5cm) the length of the fabric for the side borders. Sew to the quilt in the same manner as in step 1. Press the seams toward the outer borders.

Finishing the Quilt

1 Cut the backing and batting 4" (10cm) larger than the quilt top. Layer with the backing wrong side up, the batting and the quilt top right side up. Baste the layers together. Quilt as desired.

2 If marking a scalloped edge on the quilt, set the EZ Scallop tool at 5¼" (13.5cm) for all sides of the quilt, or mark off 5¼" (13.5cm) intervals and connect with a curve. Leave the corners square. *(Figure 6)* (See *General Instructions* for more instructions on marking a scalloped edge.)

3 From the remainder of the inner border fabric, cut six 2¼" × 42" (5.7cm × 106.5cm) strips for binding a straight edge. If binding a scalloped edge, cut the fabric into 1¼" (3.2cm) wide bias strips. (See *General Instructions* for more information on preparing binding strips.)

4 Baste on the edge of the quilt, or on the marked line if binding a scalloped edge, to hold the layers together and prevent shifting.

5 Sew the binding to the quilt with a ¼" (6mm) seam, mitering the corners. (See *General Instructions* for mitering instructions and binding a scalloped edge.)

6 Trim excess batting and backing (trim evenly to a ¼" [6mm] seam allowance) and turn the binding to the back side and stitch down by hand with matching thread.

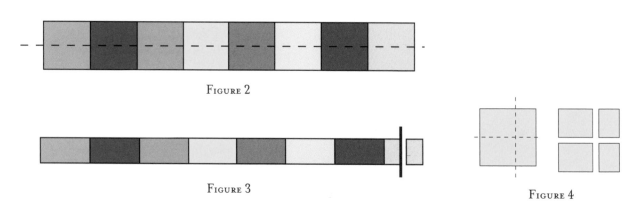

FIGURE 2

FIGURE 3

FIGURE 4

FIGURE 5

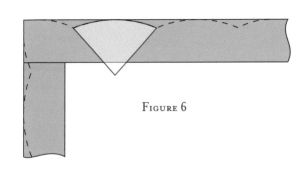

FIGURE 6

FIELD OF FLOWERS

When pieced in pastel colors, this variation on the Rail Fence block yields a field of springtime flowers. Make this sweet wall or table quilt to bring some spring sunshine into your home.

Materials

- 1 pack of 5" (12.5cm) charm squares with at least 42 squares (I used *Lazy Daisy Baskets 2* by Robert Kaufman Fabrics)
- **Background fabric:** ⅝ yd. (57.2cm)
- **Batting:** 30" × 35" (76cm × 89cm)
- **Backing:** ⅞ yd. (80cm)
- **Binding:** ¼ yd. (23cm)
- Optional: Thirty ⅜" or ⁷⁄₁₆" (9.5mm or 11.1mm) buttons for flower centers
- Hand-quilting thread

Tools

- Needle

FINISHED DIMENSIONS

26½" × 30½" (67.5cm × 80cm)
4" (10cm) finished blocks

Cutting Directions

FROM	CUT	TO YIELD
30 charms	(3) 1½" × 5" strips (3.8cm × 12.5cm)	(90) 1½" × 5" strips (3.8cm × 12.5cm)
Background	(8) 1½" × 42" strips (3.8cm × 106.5cm)	Strip sets
	(3) 1½" × 42" strips (3.8cm × 106.5cm)	Inner border
Binding	(3) 2¼" × 42" strips (5.5cm × 106.5cm)	Binding

Assembling the Blocks

1 Sew 2 of the 1½" × 5" (3.8cm × 12.5cm) print strips to a background strip to make a strip set. Repeat for each of the 30 prints. Press toward the print strips. (*Figure 1*) Cut the units apart.

2 Cut each of the strip sets from step 1 into two 2½" × 2½" (6.5cm × 6.5cm) units. (*Figure 2*)

3 Sew 4 matching units from step 2 together to make a flower block. Twist the center seam to open. (See *General Instructions* for directions on this technique.) Make 30 blocks. At this point they should measure 4½" (11.5cm) square. (*Figure 3*)

Assembling the Quilt

1 Arrange the blocks in 6 rows of 5 blocks and sew. Press the row seams in alternate directions. (*Figure 4*)

2 Sew the rows together, pressing the seams open or all in one direction.

Borders

1 Measure and trim two 1½" (3.8cm) wide inner background borders the width of the quilt. Sew to the top and bottom of the quilt. Press the seams toward the borders. Repeat for the side borders.

2 Cut one of the remaining charm squares into four 2½" (6.5cm) squares for the corners. Set aside.

3 Cut the remaining 11 charm squares into three 1½" × 5" (3.8cm × 12.5cm) strips each. Sew those strips and the remaining strips from the blocks into 13 strips sets of 4. You will have some strips left over. (*Figure 5*)

4 Sew 6 units from step 3 together for the top of the quilt. Remove 2 strips. Press the seams in one direction. Cut the pieced border lengthwise into 2 borders. The borders now measure 2½" × 22½" (6cm × 57cm). Sew one to the top of the quilt and one to the bottom of the quilt. Press the seams toward the inner border. (*Figure 6*)

NOTE: If needed, adjust the pieced borders by taking in or letting out a few seams to make the borders fit the quilt.

5 In the same manner, sew 7 units from step 3 together for the sides of the quilt. (You will have some units left over.) Remove 2 strips. Cut the pieced border lengthwise into 2 borders. (*Figure 7*) Sew corner squares (from step 2) to the ends of the borders. Press the seams toward the corner squares. The side borders with corner squares should measure 2½" × 30½" (6cm × 77cm). Sew to the sides of the quilt. Press toward the inner border.

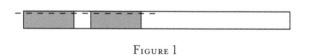

FIGURE 1

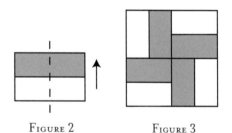

FIGURE 2 FIGURE 3

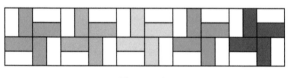

FIGURE 4

FIGURE 5

Finishing the Quilt

1 Layer the backing wrong side up, the batting and the quilt top right side up. Baste, then quilt as desired. The quilt shown was machine quilting using a meandering stitch in the background areas and quilted in the ditch in the pieced border.

2 Before binding, hand-baste a scant ¼" (6mm) from the edge of the quilt to hold the layers together and prevent shifting.

3 Prepare the binding by sewing the ends together with diagonal seams press open. Fold the binding in half, wrong sides together, and press to make a double binding. Sew to the quilt with a ¼" (6mm) seam, mitering the corners. (See *General Instructions* for more instruction on binding.)

4 Trim the excess batting and backing, turn the binding to the back side of the quilt and stitch down by hand with matching thread.

5 Sew buttons to the center of each flower, through all the layers.

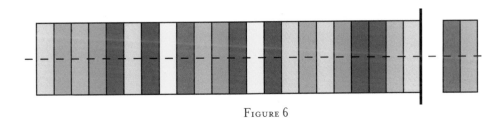

Figure 6

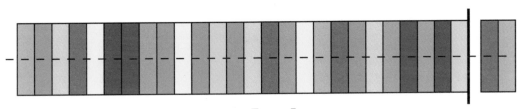

Figure 7

LAKE COUNTRY

This quilt may look complicated, but it is really quite easy to assemble. Worried about sewing all those triangles? Pre-cut strips and the Easy Angle tool make them a breeze to cut and sew. And remember, practice makes perfect. By the time you finish this quilt, you will be an expert!

Materials

- I jelly roll with at least 40 strips, both light and dark colors (I used *Lake Country* from Robert Kaufman Fabrics)
- **NOTE**: If you don't have enough light prints in the jelly roll, cut some 2½"(6.5cm) strips from your stash or buy extra fat quarters.
- **Background Print:** 2 yds. (1.8m)
- **Binding:** ⅝ yd. (57.2cm)
- **Backing:** 3¼ yds. (3m)
- **Batting:** Twin size
- Optional: Hand-quilting thread

Tools

- EZ Angle (mini [EZ Quilting no. 882188] 4½" [11.5cm], EZ Quilting no. 882670179A or 6½" [16.5cm] [EZ Quilting no. 8823759A] size) or traceable template provided
- Optional: Needle

FINISHED DIMENSIONS
53½" × 67½" (136cm × 172cm)
6" (15cm) finished blocks

Cutting Directions

FROM	CUT	TO YIELD
Background	(12) 2½" × 42" strips (6.5cm × 106.5cm)	(189) 2½" (6.5cm) squares
	(24) 1½" × 42" strips (3.8cm × 106.5cm)	(63) 1½" × 7½" (3.8cm × 19cm) sashes
		(63) 1½" × 6½" (3.8cm × 16.5cm) sashes
Light Prints	(15) 2½" × 42 (6.5cm × 106.5cm) jelly roll strips	378 EZ Angle triangles*
Dark Prints	(23) 2½" × 42 (6.5mm × 106.5cm) jelly roll strips	(32) 2½" × 7½" (6.5cm × 19cm) rectangles for borders
		(4) 2½" (6.5cm) squares for corners
		378 Easy Angle triangles
Binding	(7) 2¼" × 42" strips (5.5cm × 106.5cm)	Binding

Assembling the Blocks

1 Sew all the light and dark triangles together in pairs to make 378 triangle squares. Press the seams toward the dark triangle. Trim dog ears. At this point the squares should measure 2½" (6.5cm). (*Figure 1*)

2 Using 3 background squares and a variety of step 1 triangle squares, piece a block as shown. At this point the block should measure 6½" (16.5cm) square. Repeat to make a total of 63 blocks. (*Figures 2 and 3*)

3 Using the 1½" × 6½" (3.8cm × 16.5cm) sashing strips, sew to the right side of each of the blocks exactly as shown. Press the seams toward the sashing strips. (*Figure 4*)

4 Using the 1½" × 7½" (3.8cm × 19cm) sashing strips, sew to the blocks from step 3 exactly as shown. Press. At this point the blocks should measure 7½" (19cm) square. (*Figure 5*)

Tip: To save time at the sewing machine, layer light and dark 2½"-wide (6.5cm-wide) strips, right sides together, to cut the triangles. They will then be ready to chain piece.

Assembling the Quilt

1 Arrange the blocks in a row as shown. Sew together and press the seams toward the sashing strips. Make 9 rows. (*Figure 6*)

2 Reverse every other row before sewing the rows together. Sew the seams, pressing the row seams open. (*Figure 7*)

Refer to the flat shot of the Lake Country quilt on page 111.

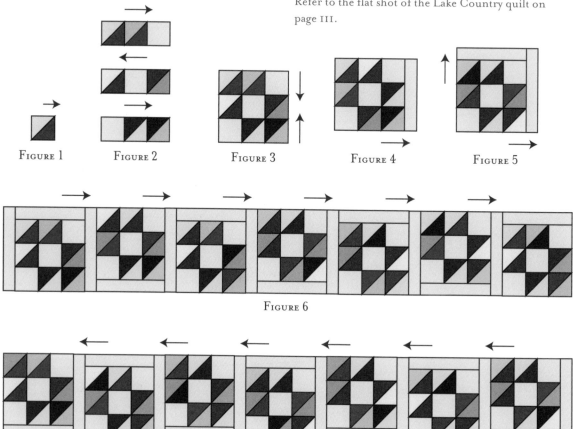

FIGURE 1   FIGURE 2   FIGURE 3   FIGURE 4   FIGURE 5

FIGURE 6

FIGURE 7

Border

1 Join 7 dark 2½" × 7½" (6.5cm × 19cm) rectangles end to end. Press the seams all one direction. Make 2 borders. Sew to the top and bottom of the quilt. Press toward the borders. *(Figure 8)*

2 Join 9 dark 2½" × 7½" (6.5cm × 19cm) rectangles end to end for the side borders. Press the seams all one direction. Add the 2½" (6.5cm) squares at both ends of the borders. Press toward the long rectangles. Sew the borders to the sides of the quilt, pressing the seams toward the borders. *(Figure 9)*

Finishing the Quilt

1 Piece the backing, then layer the backing wrong side up, the batting and the quilt top right side up. Baste, then quilt as desired.

2 Before binding, use a walking foot to machine-baste a scant ¼" (6mm) from the edge of the quilt to hold the layers together and prevent shifting.

3 Prepare the binding by joining the short ends of the binding strips with diagonal seams pressed open. Fold the binding in half, wrong sides together, and press to make a double binding.

4 Sew to the quilt with a ¼" (6mm) seam, mitering the corners. (For more information on making binding and binding a quilt, see *General Information*.)

5 Trim excess batting and backing; turn the binding to the back side of the quilt and stitch down by hand with matching thread.

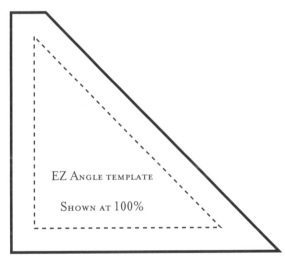

EZ Angle template

Shown at 100%

Figure 8

Figure 9

STAINED GLASS FANS

The sweet little fans on this quilt are easy to make, and are accented by a pieced border made with scraps. This fan quilt is quick to make, and you will have enough charm squares to make two quilts!

Materials

- 1 charm pack with at least forty-two 5" [12.5cm] squares (I used *Sunstreaks* by Robert Kaufman Fabrics)
- **Black fabric:** ¾ yd. (68.6cm)
- **Batting:** 22" × 26" (56cm × 66cm) rectangle
- **Backing:** ⅔ yd. (60.4cm)
- **Optiona:** Hand-quilting thread

Tools

- 30° Triangle template (EZ Quilting no. 8829418A) or Mini 30° Triangle tool (EZ Quilting no. 882181) or traceable template provided
- Companion Angle triangle (EZ Quilting no. 882670139A) or traceable template provided
- Optional: Needle

FINISHED DIMENSIONS
19" × 23" (48.5cm × 58.5cm)
3½" (9cm) finished blocks

Cutting Directions

Choose 18 of the 5" (12.5cm) charm squares to use for the fans. Cut 1½" × 5" (3.8cm × 12.5cm) off of one side of the square. Set aside for border.

From each of the remaining 3½" × 5" (9cm 12.5cm) rectangles, cut three 30° triangles for a total of 54 triangles.

From the black fabric, cut:

Two 4" × 42" (10cm × 106.5cm) strips; cut into twenty 4" (10.2cm) squares

One 3" × 42" (7.5cm × 106.5cm) strip; cut into 10 Companion Angles.

One 5" × 42" (12.5cm × 106.5cm) strip; cut into sixteen 1½" × 5" (3.8cm × 12.5cm) rectangles for the borders and four 2¼" (5.5cm) squares for border corners

Three 2¼" × 42" (5.5cm × 106.5cm) strips for binding

Assembling the Fan Blocks

1 Fold each of the 30° triangles, right sides together at the widest edge. With a short stitch length, sew a ¼" (6mm) seam across the top end. Trim the folded corner, then turn to make the folded point. Press with the seam centered in the middle of the triangle. Repeat for all 54 triangles. *(Figures 1 and 2)*

2 Place two triangles right sides together, matching side edges. Sew a ¼" (6mm) seam, back-stitching at the folded edges as shown. Press to the left. Repeat for 18 pairs. *(Figure 3)*

3 Using the pairs created in step 2, sew a third triangle to the units as before, creating a small fan. Repeat to make 18 fans. *(Figure 4)*

4 Place a fan on the corner of a 4" (10cm) black square. Align the corner and edges. Pin in place, then appliqué the folded points to the background by hand or machine. Trim away the black background from under the fan, trimming ¼" (6mm) from the appliqué stitching. Repeat to make 18 blocks. *(Figure 5)*

Assembling the Quilt

1 Arrange the fan blocks in diagonal rows, with the fans pointing up. Place the Companion Angle triangles along the edges. Cut the 2 remaining 4" (10cm) black squares in half on the diagonal. Place those triangles at the corners of the quilt. *(Figure 6)*

2 Sew the blocks and triangles together in diagonal rows, alternating the direction the seams are pressed in each row. Sew the rows together and add the corner triangles last. Press all of the row seams in one direction. Wait to trim the edges.

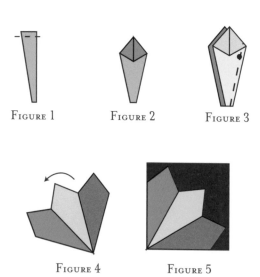

FIGURE 1   FIGURE 2   FIGURE 3

FIGURE 4   FIGURE 5

FIGURE 6

Border

1 Alternate the 1½" × 5" (3.8cm × 12.5cm) colored rectangles with the black 1½" × 5" (3.8cm × 12.5cm) rectangles and sew. Sew one border with 8 colored rectangles and 7 black rectangles. Press all the seams in one direction. Cut the strips in half to make two 2¼"-wide (5.5cm-wide) borders. *(Figure 7)*

2 Repeat step 1 to make a second border with 10 colored rectangles and 9 black rectangles. Press the seams in one direction. Cut in half lengthwise to make two 2¼" (5.5cm) borders. *(Figure 8)*

3 Measure and trim the sides of the quilt the same length as the step 2 side borders. Trim the bottom of the quilt only enough to straighten the edge, trimming more off the top of the quilt. *(Figure 9)*

4 Trim the width of the quilt to the same measurement as the step 1 border.

5 Sew the top and bottom borders to the quilt. Press toward the inner borders.

6 Sew the black 2¼" (5.5cm) squares to both ends of the side borders. Press toward the pieced borders. Sew to the sides of the quilt. Press the seams toward inner the borders.

Finishing the Quilt

1 Layer the backing, wrong side up, the batting, then the quilt top right side up. Baste, then quilt as desired. The quilt shown was machine quilted in a small meander in the black background. It was also stitched in the ditch around the fans and between the colored rectangles in the border.

2 Before binding, hand-baste a scant ¼" (6mm) from the edge of the quilt to hold the layers together.

3 Prepare the binding strips by joining with diagonal seams pressed open. Fold the binding in half, wrong sides together, and press to make a double binding.

4 Sew the binding to the quilt with a ¼" (6mm) seam, mitering the corners. (For more instruction on binding a quilt, see *General Instructions*)

5 Trim the excess batting and backing, turn the binding to the back side and stitch down by hand with matching thread.

FIGURE 7

FIGURE 8

FIGURE 9

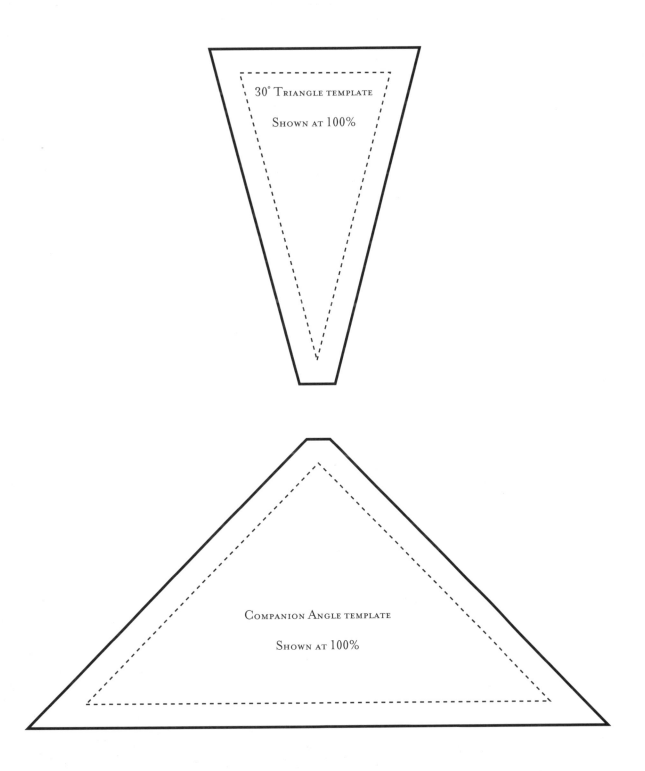

30° Triangle template

Shown at 100%

Companion Angle template

Shown at 100%

THIMBLE QUILT

What can you make with those sample 2½" (6.5cm) mini charm squares? This easy *Thimble Quilt* is the answer. Quick to cut and sew, the project is simple enough for a beginner, and oh-so-pretty when finished!

Materials

- 3 mini charm packs with at least ninety-one 2½" (6.5cm) squares. (I used *La Belle Fleur* by French General for Moda.)
- **Border:** ⅓ yd. (30.5cm)
- **Binding:** Fat quarter or ⅓ yd. (30.5cm)
- **Backing:** ⅝ yd. (57.2cm)
- Hand-quilting thread

Tools

- Traceable template provided or Mini Dresden tool (EZ Quilting no. 882819) or Easy Dresden tool (EZ Quilting no. 8829306A)
- Easy Scallop (EZ Quilting no. 8827354A)
- Needle

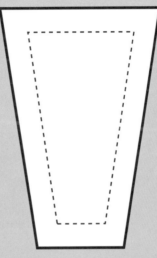

EASY DRESDEN TEMPLATE

SHOWN AT 100%

FINISHED DIMENSIONS

19" × 23" (48.5cm × 58.5cm)

Cutting Directions

FROM	CUT	TO YIELD
Ninety-one 2½" (6.5cm) squares	91 wedges with template or tool (see illustration below)	
Border	(2) 4" × 42" strips (10cm × 106.5cm)	outer borders
Binding	1¼" (3.2cm) single bias binding	

Assembling the Quilt

1 Alternating light and dark wedges, arrange 7 rows of 13 wedges. (*Figure 1*)

2 Sew the wedges together in each row, slightly off-setting the wedges as shown. Press the seams toward the darker wedges. (*Figure 2*)

3 Pin and sew 2 rows together, matching the seam intersections. Press the seam open. Repeat for all the rows. (*Figure 1*)

4 Using a ruler and rotary cutter, trim the side edges of the quilt straight, trimming as little as possible. (*Figure 3*)

5 Measure and cut 2 borders the length of the sides of the quilt. Sew to the sides of the quilt. Press the seams toward the borders. Repeat for the top and bottom borders.

Cutting wedges

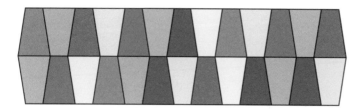

Figure 1

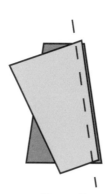

Figure 2

Figure 3

82

Finishing the Quilt

1 Cut the batting and backing 4" (10cm) larger than the quilt top. Layer the backing wrong side up, the batting and the quilt top right side up. Baste, then quilt as desired. The quilt shown was hand-quilted in the ditch on all sides of the wedges. The border was quilted in straight lines.

2 Using the EZ Scallop tool set at 4¼" (11cm) (or mark intervals of 4¼" (11cm) and connect with a curve), mark scallops on the edges of the quilt, leaving the corners square. (Figure 4)

3 Baste using a walking foot on the machine or by hand on the marked line to hold the layers of the quilt together and prevent shifting.

4 Prepare the bias binding according to the binding instructions in *General Instructions*. Sew to the quilt with a ¼" (6mm) seam using your ¼" [6mm] machine foot. Also see *General Instructions* for stitching a scalloped edge and mitering corners.

5 Trim the excess batting and backing to ¼" (6mm) from the sewing line and fold the binding over on the back side of the quilt, covering the stitching line. Fold a pleat into the V of the scallop. Stitch the binding in place by hand with matching thread.

Figure 4

THE MANLY QUILT

This book is dedicated to my husband, who has suffered through the delivery and birth of numerous books with me. My usual quilt color palette is pretty and pastel, but I wanted to make something for the man in my life. The dark flannels I used have the appearance of wool and were a perfect choice for a manly quilt.

Materials

- 16 fat quarters (I used *Woolies Flannel* from Maywood Studio); half light prints, half dark prints
- **Sashing, Border and Binding:** 2⅔ yds. (2.4m)
- **Backing:** 4 yds. (3.7m)
- **Batting:** Twin size (72" × 96" [1.8m × 2.4m])

Tools

- EZ Angle (EZ Quilting no. 8823759) or see instructions under Cutting Directions

FINISHED DIMENSIONS
68" × 81" (172.7cm × 205.7cm)

Cutting Directions

Tip: Before cutting the triangles, sort the fat quarters into 8 light and 8 dark. To cut the strips, pair one light and one dark strip, right sides together, and cut the triangles. They will be ready to chain sew.

FROM	CUT	TO YIELD
Each fat quarter	Three 5½" × 21" (14cm × 53.5cm) strips	17 Easy Angle triangles*
Border fabric	Six 3½" × 68" (9cm × 172.7cm) strips	Sashing and side borders
	Two 8½" × 70" (21.5cm × 177.8cm) strips	Top and bottom borders
Binding	1¾" (4.5cm) bias strips	325" (8.3m) single bias binding
	(use remainder of border fabric for binding)	

*If not using the EZ Angle, cut eight or nine 5⅞" (14.9cm) squares from each fat quarter; cut once on the diagonal. You may need an additional fat quarter or two if your fat quarters are less than 18" × 21" (45.5cm × 53.5cm).

Assembling the Flying Geese

1 Place a light and a dark triangle, right sides together, and sew on the diagonal edge. Press the seams open to reduce bulk. Make 130 triangle-squares. At this point they should measure 5½" (14cm) square. Trim dog ears. (*Figure 1*)

2 Sew 2 triangle-squares from step 1 together to form a Flying Geese unit. Press the seam open. Make 65 Flying Geese units. At this point the units should measure 5½" × 10½" (14cm × 26.5cm). (*Figure 2*)

3 Sew the Flying Geese units together in 5 long rows of 13 geese each. Press the seams open. At this point, the rows should measure 10½" × 65½" (26.5cm × 166.4cm). If not, take an average of the 5 rows. Trim the six 3½" (9cm) wide sashing strips to 65½" (166.4cm) or the length of your rows.

4 Sew the sashing strips between each row of flying geese. The rows may point in opposite directions as shown, or all the same direction—your choice!

Sew sashing rows on the sides of the quilt top as well. Press all the seams open. (*Figure 3*)

5 Trim the two 8½"-wide (21.5cm-wide) border strips to the width of the quilt. Sew to the top and bottom of the quilt. Press the seams open. (*Figure 3*)

Finishing the Quilt

1 Layer the backing wrong side up, the batting and the quilt top right side up. Baste, then quilt as desired. The quilt shown was machine quilted in an all-over design.

2 Before binding, baste ¼" (6mm) from the edge of the quilt to hold the layers together. Cut the single bias binding from the remainder of the border fabric.

Piece together with diagonal seams pressed open. (See *General Instructions* for more information on bias binding.

3 Sew the binding to the quilt with a ⅜" (1cm) seam allowance, mitering the corners. Trim off the excess batting and backing; turn the binding to the back side, tuck under ⅜" (1cm) and stitch down by hand with matching thread. (See *General Instructions* for more information on binding.)

FIGURE 1

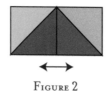

FIGURE 2

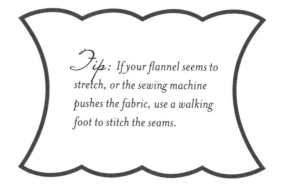

Tip: If your flannel seems to stretch, or the sewing machine pushes the fabric, use a walking foot to stitch the seams.

FIGURE 3

SUMMERTIME QUILT

Ah, summertime. Picnics, fireworks, fishing, vacations. What could be better? Seeing a bundle of red, white and blue fabrics in batiks inspired me to make a patriotic quilt to celebrate the Fourth of July and my favorite season—summer.

Materials

- 2 jelly rolls (I used *Artisan Batiks: Color Source* by Robert Kaufman [red, white and blue])
- **White print:** 1⅜ yds. (1.3m)
- **Red print for inner border and binding:** 1 yd. (91cm)
- **Backing:** 3⅓ yds.
- **Batting:** Twin Size

  OR substitute the following for the 2 jelly rolls:
- **White:** 3 fat quarters or ten 2½" × 42" (6.5cm × 106.5cm) strips
- **Red:** 3 fat quarters or eight 2½" × 42" (6.5cm × 106.5cm) strips
- **Blue:** 9 fat quarters or thirty-one 2½" × 42" (6.5cm × 106.5cm) strips

Tools

- EZ Angle (EZ Quilting no. 8823759A) or Mini Easy Angle (EZ Quilting no. 882188) or traceable template provided
- **Note:** You must use the EZ Angle or the template provided for the triangles. Otherwise, your finished triangles will be too small.
- Optional: EZ Scallop (EZ Quilting no. 8823754A)

FINISHED DIMENSIONS

56" × 75" (142.2cm × 190.5cm)

8" (20.5cm) blocks set 4 blocks by 6 rows

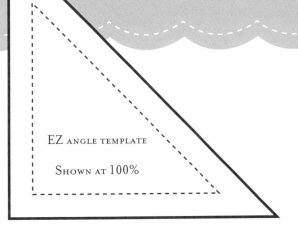

EZ ANGLE TEMPLATE

SHOWN AT 100%

Cutting Directions

FROM	CUT	TO YIELD
White yardage	Fifteen 2½" × 42" (6.5cm × 106.5cm) strips	58 sashings 2½" × 8½" (6.5cm × 21.5cm)
	Three 2½" × 42" (6.5cm × 106.5cm) strips	Forty-eight 2½" (6.5cm) squares
White jelly roll strips	Six 2½" × 42" (6.5cm × 106.5cm) strips	Strip sets
	Four 2½" × 42" (6.5cm × 106.5cm) strips	96 Easy Angle triangles*
Blue jelly roll strips	Three 2½" × 42" (6.5cm × 106.5cm) strips	Forty-eight 2½" (6.5cm) squares for blocks
	Two 2½" × 42" (6.5cm × 106.5cm) strips	Eighteen 2½" (6.5cm) squares for cornerstones
	Four 2½" × 42" (6.5cm × 106.5cm) strips	96 Easy Angle triangles*
	Twenty-two 2½" × 42" (6.5cm × 106.5cm) strips	One-hundred-thirty-two 2½" × 6½" (6.5cm × 16.5cm) border strips
Red jelly roll strips	Six 2½" × 42" (6.5cm × 106.5cm) strips	Strip sets
	Two 2½" × 42" (6.5cm × 106.5cm) strips	Seventeen 2½" (6.5cm) squares for cornerstones
Red yardage	Six 1½" × 42" (3.8cm × 106.5cm) strips	Inner border
	1¼" (3.2cm) bias binding strips	300" (7.6m) of bias binding

* Layer the blue and white/cream print strips right sides together and cut Easy Angle triangles. They will then be ready to chain sew.

Assembling the Blocks

1 Sew the red and white strips together in pairs. Press toward the red. Repeat to make 6 strip sets. Cut into ninety-six 2½" (6.5cm) units. (*Figure 1*)

2 Sew 2 units from step 1 together to make 48 four-patches. Twist the last seam to open a few threads at the center, making all the seam allowances spin around the center. (See *General Instructions* for information on this technique.) At this point the four-patches should measure 4½" (11.5cm) square. (*Figure 2*)

3 Sew all the blue and white triangles together on the diagonal edge. Press toward the blue triangles. Sew a triangle square and a white square together as shown. Press toward the white square. Make 48. (*Figures 3 and 4*)

4 Sew a blue square and a triangle square together as shown. Press the seam toward the blue square. Make 48. (*Figure 5*)

5 Sew the step 3 and step 4 units together in pairs. Twist the last seam to open a few threads at the center, making all the seam allowances spin around the center. Make 48. (*Figure 6*) At this point the units should measure 4½" square.

6 Sew the Figure 2 and Figure 6 units together to make pairs. Press toward the red and white four-patches. Sew the pairs together to make 24 blocks. Twist the last seam so the seams spin around the center. At this point the blocks should measure 8½" (21.5cm) square. (*Figures 7 and 8*)

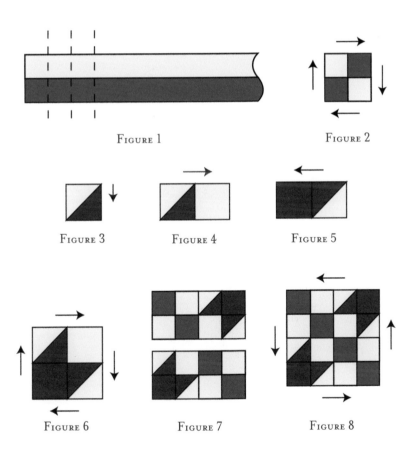

FIGURE 1

FIGURE 2

FIGURE 3

FIGURE 4

FIGURE 5

FIGURE 6

FIGURE 7

FIGURE 8

Assembling the Quilt

1 Sew 4 blocks together in rows with white/cream sashing strips between the blocks and at both ends of the rows. Press the seams toward the sashing. Make 6 rows. *(Figure 9)*

2 Sew 4 horizontal sashing rows, using 3 blue cornerstones, 2 red cornerstones and 4 sashing strips. Press the seams toward the sashing strips. *(Figure 10)*

3 Sew 3 horizontal sashing rows, using 2 blue cornerstones, 3 red cornerstones and 4 sashing strips. Press toward the sashing strips. *(Figure 11)*

4 Sew the steps 1, 2 and 3 rows together as shown in the photo on the next page. Press the seams toward the sashing rows.

Borders

1 Measure, piece and sew the 1½" (3.8cm) red inner borders to the quilt top.

2 Sew 28 blue 2½" × 6½" (6.5cm × 16.5cm) strips together on the long edges to make a top border. Press all seams in one direction. Repeat for the bottom border.

3 Sew 38 blue 2½" × 6½" (6.5cm × 16.5cm) strips together on the long edges to make side borders. Press all seams in one direction. Repeat for the second side border.

4 Center and sew the blue pieced border strips to the top and bottom of the quilt, extending the edges beyond the quilt top for mitering later. There should be exactly 3 border strips extra on each end of the quilt. Adjust seams in order for the border to fit exactly. Repeat for the side borders. Miter the corners. (See *General Instructions* for information on mitering corners.)

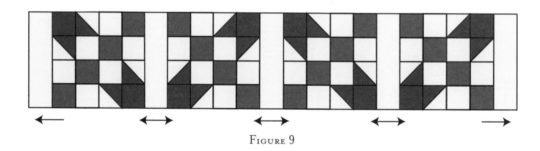

FIGURE 9

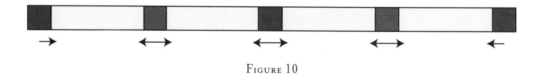

FIGURE 10

FIGURE 11

Finishing the Quilt

1 Layer, baste and quilt as desired. After quilting, mark 5" (12.5cm) scallops using the small Easy Scallop tool, reversing every other one to make a wavy edge. Alternately, mark 5" (12.5cm) intervals and connect with a curved line. Mark the waves starting at the corners and working towards the center. Adjust the center wave as needed. The scallops will overlap at the corners, creating a rounded corner. (See *General Instructions* for more instruction.)

2 After marking the wavy edge, baste by hand or with a walking foot on the marked line. Do not cut on the line.

3 Prepare the 1¼" (3.2cm) red single bias binding by joining the ends with diagonal seams pressed open. Sew the binding to the quilt with a ¼" (6mm) seam, aligning the binding with the marked line, sewing ¼" (6mm) below the marked line, and easing it around the curves. Trim the excess batting and backing evenly to ¼" (6mm). Turn the binding under on the back side and stitch down by hand with matching thread. (See *General Instructions* for more instruction on cutting, preparing and sewing a bias binding on a curved edge.)

General Instructions

CHOOSING FABRIC

Publishing a book is a long process. If the fabrics used in these projects are no longer available, don't despair! Choose similar fabrics if you like the original quilt, or be daring and choose a different colorway for an interesting variation. Whatever fabrics you choose, buy the best quality. Quality fabrics will be easier to sew, and you will have a better finished product. The colors will last longer, and the fabric will hold up well to wear and tear. **Note:** Jelly roll strips are 2½" × 42" (6.5cm × 106.5cm). You can substitute fat quarters or scraps for the jelly roll strips. Honeybuns are 1½" × 42" (3.8cm × 106.5cm) strips of fabric.

PREPARING THE FABRIC

You may choose to prewash your fabric—or not. It is a personal decision. The fabric will lose some body, and you may have some shrinkage and unraveling. You can restore the body with a little spray starch or fabric sizing, but don't leave such products in the finished quilt long-term—they may attract dirt and bugs. You can test a fabric for color bleeding by spritzing a small area with water and then ironing it, right sides together, with a white fabric. If there is color transference, it would be safer to prewash. Ironing the folds out of the fabric is a necessary step for accurate cutting.

CUTTING

Accuracy in cutting is important for the pieces to fit together properly in your quilt. Some tips for accurate cutting:
• Work in good light—daylight, if possible.
• Iron the fabrics before cutting.
• Cut only two layers of fabric at a time. Any time saved in cutting more layers will be lost when trying to fit together the inaccurate pieces.
• Keep your tools from slipping. Use a film or sandpaper that adheres to the back of the tools.
• Use a sharp rotary cutter and a good mat. Mats and cutting blades do wear out over time, so replace them as needed.

USING THE TOOLS

For most of the projects in this book, you will need a self-healing mat, rotary cutter, various sizes of quilting rulers, a sewing machine, scissors, pins and other notions. These items are all easily found at your local craft retailers.

Use a rotary cutter only on a self-healing mat to avoid damage to your cutting surface. When cutting, push away from you with the blade—this will help minimize the potential for injury. When cutting a straight edge, slide the rotary cutter blade down the edge of an acrylic quilting ruler, being sure to keep your fingers out of the way.

Any additional tool requirements or suggestions are found with each project.

SEWING

Sewing accurate ¼" (6mm) seams is important! If at all possible, find a ¼" foot for your sewing machine, made specifically for quilt piecing. They are well worth the small investment. A walking foot is also recommended for basting and straight-line quilting.
If you have problems with the feed dogs chewing up your fabric, try these tricks to tame them:
• Insert a new needle—a sharps or quilting needle. An 80/12 would be a good size.
• Clean and oil your sewing machine. Particularly clean under the throat plate.
• Chain sew whenever possible.
• Begin and end with a scrap of fabric.

Try This!

Try this quick check to see if you are sewing an exact ¼" (6mm) seam allowance: Cut three 1½" × 3½" (3.8cm × 9cm) strips. Sew them together on the long edges. Press. The square should now measure 3½" (9cm). If not, adjust your seam allowance. (Also check that you have pressed correctly.)

UNSEWING

It's a fact of life: Mistakes happen. Use a seam ripper when necessary. Strive for perfection and then learn from your mistakes, but also forgive yourself for not being perfect. The Amish place a deliberate mistake in a quilt as a *humility block* because they believe only God is perfect.

PRESSING

Remember that the purpose of pressing is to make the seam, unit, block and quilt top as flat as possible. Iron from the right side whenever possible. Follow the pressing arrows given in the directions. If you follow these, most, if not all, of your seams will alternate for a flat piece.

BATTING

The type of batting you use is a personal choice. Cotton batting will give you a flat, traditional look and will shrink a bit when you wash the quilt, resulting in a slightly puckered look. Cotton batting is more difficult to hand quilt, but it will machine quilt nicely because the layers of the quilt will not shift.

Polyester batting has a bit more loft (puffiness) than a cotton batting and is easier to hand quilt. However, it is more slippery, which can cause shifting when machine quilting. Combination poly-and-cotton battings can give you the best qualities of both and are a good choice for hand- and machine-quilting.

QUILTING

After you have finished your quilt top, it's time to consider quilting. Some tops need to be marked for quilting before they are basted together with the batting and background fabric, others while they are being quilted. Whichever marking device you use, test it on scraps of fabric from the project to check if it can be easily removed.

Create your quilt sandwich by layering the batting between the quilt top and the backing fabric and basting the layers together with safety pins or thread 4" (10cm) apart. The batting and backing should be cut at least 4" (10cm) larger than the quilt top.

Some of the quilts in this book were hand-quilted, while others were machine-quilted on a sewing machine, and still others were sent out to a long-arm quilter. Feel free to create your own quilting designs.

TWISTING THE SEAM

Try this trick whenever you have any type of four-patch unit. It will make the center seam intersection lie flatter.

1. Before pressing the last seam on a four-patch, grasp the seam with both hands about 1" (2.5cm) from the center seam. Twist in opposite directions, opening a few threads in the seam. (*Figure 1*)

2. Press one seam in one direction and the other seam in the opposite direction. In the center you will see a tiny four-patch appear, and the center now lies very flat. (*Figure 2*)

FIGURE 1

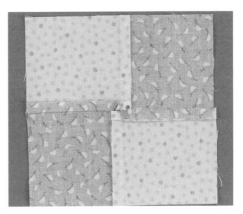

FIGURE 2

BINDING

Generally I use double bias or double straight-of-grain binding for any straight edges and single bias binding for curved edges.

1. To cut bias binding, trim off the selvages and trim both the bottom and top edges of the fabric chosen for the binding. Using the 45° line on your long ruler, align it with the edge of the fabric and cut off the corner at a 45° angle. The fabric should be opened, cutting through a single layer. *(Figure 1)*

2. Set the corner aside for another use and cut binding strips from the remainder of the fabric *(Figure 2a)*, folding the fabric along the cut edge as needed to shorten the cut. *(Figure 2b)*

3. After the strips have been cut, join the angled ends exactly as shown *(Figure 3a)*. Sew from the V at the top of the strip to the V at the bottom of the strip (the seam allowance does not have to be ¼" [6mm]). Sew all the strips in this manner to make a continuous binding strip. Press the seams open and trim seams to ¼". *(Figure 3b)*

4. To make a double binding, fold the binding in half, wrong sides together, and press. *(Figure 4)*

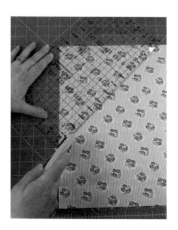

FIGURE 1

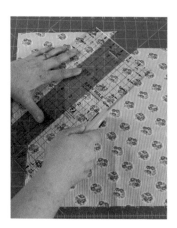

FIGURE 2A

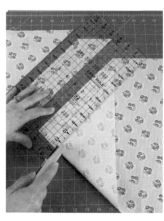

FIGURE 2B

FIGURE 3A

FIGURE 3B

FIGURE 4

MITERING CORNERS ON BINDING

1. When the quilting is completed, baste a scant ¼" (6mm) around the perimeter of the quilt to prevent the layers from shifting while the binding is being sewn on. This prevents the edge from stretching. Leave the excess batting and backing in place until after the binding is sewn on so you can trim off the exact amount needed to completely fill the binding. *(Figure 1)*

2. Begin sewing the binding to the quilt in the middle of one side, matching the raw edges of the binding to the raw edge of the quilt top. Leave a 6"–8" (15cm–20.5cm) tail at the beginning. *(Figure 2)*

3. To miter a corner, stitch to within a seam's allowance from the corner, stop and backstitch. *(Figure 3)*

4. Remove the quilt from under the presser foot and trim the threads. Turn the quilt 90° and pull the binding straight up, forming a 45° angle at the corner. *(Figure 4)*

5. Fold the binding back down, with the fold on the previously stitched edge of the quilt. Begin stitching at the fold. This will build in enough extra binding to turn the corner. *(Figure 5)*

6. For corners that are not square (such as on a table runner), stitch the first edge, stop a seam's allowance from the corner and remove the quilt from under the presser foot. Pull the binding straight up and then fold it back down along the next edge. The fold should now come right to the corner of the quilt. It will not align with the previous edge as in a square corner, but rather at right angles to the next edge. Begin stitching at the previous edge.

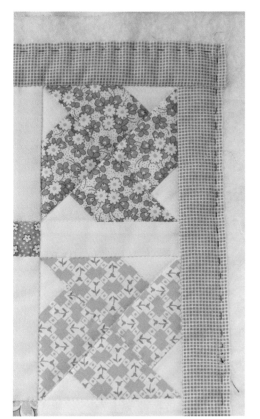

FIGURE 1

FIGURE 2

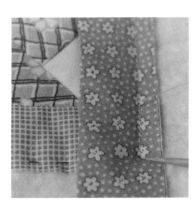

FIGURE 3

FIGURE 4

FIGURE 5

"PERFECT-FIT" BINDING

1. When you are within 8"–10" (20.5cm–25.5cm) of where you began binding, stop stitching. Remove the quilt from under the presser foot and trim the threads. (*Figure 1*)

2. On a flat surface, have the binding ends meet in the center of that unstitched area, leaving a scant ¼" (6mm) between them. Fold the ends over and crease them where they almost meet. (*Figure 2*)

3. Cut one end off at the fold. Then, using the end you have just cut off (open it, if it is a double binding), use it to measure a binding's width away from the fold. Cut off the second end at that measurement. (*Figure 3*)

4. Join the ends at right angles with right sides together. Stitch a diagonal seam. (*Figure 4*) Check if the seam is sewn correctly before trimming it to a ¼" (6mm) seam allowance. Finger press the seam open and reposition the binding on the quilt.

5. Finish stitching the binding to the edge of the quilt. (*Figure 5*)

6. Trim the excess batting and backing. On the top side of the quilt, press the binding away from the edge of the quilt to make it easier to stitch on the back side. (*Figure 6*)

7. On the back side of the quilt, fold the binding over the edge so it covers the stitching line. Hand sew or machine sew the binding in place with matching thread. (*Figure 7*)

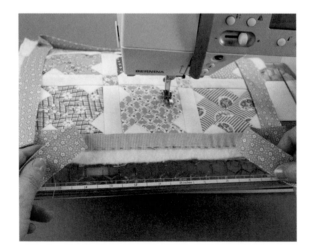

Figure 1

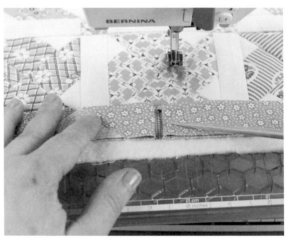

Figure 2

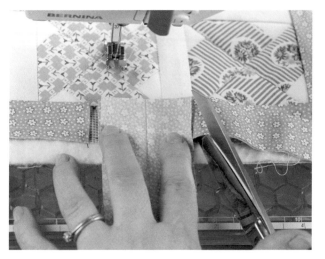

FIGURE 3

FIGURE 4

FIGURE 5

FIGURE 6

FIGURE 7

Try This!

- Use appliqué sharps , which are a type of hand needle, to hand-stitch the binding. These long, thin needles are designed for this type of stitching.
- When stitching the binding down by hand, keep the body of the quilt away from you, holding only the binding edge. You'll find it easier to stitch.
- Use binding clips instead of stick pins to hold the binding edge down for sewing and to avoid poking yourself!

FIGURE 1

FIGURE 2

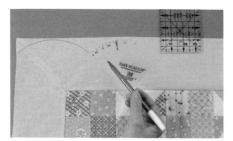

FIGURE 3

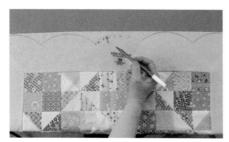

FIGURE 4

1. Measure the quilt border from edge to edge. (*Figure 1*)

2. The next step is to choose the *number of scallops* you want to create. To do this, simply take your finger and "air draw" the scallops along that edge. How many scallops did you draw? (*Figure 2*)

3. Take the length of the quilt edge and divide by the *number of scallops*. That will yield the *size* of the scallops.

4. Round the answer from step 3 to the nearest quarter inch (6mm). Set your EZ Scallop tool to that measurement.

5. Begin marking at the corner of the quilt. (You can mark right to the edge, as you will be sewing ¼" (6mm) below the marked line.) Mark the first scallop with Easy Scallop, making sure you have the same amount of indent at each end of the tool. If not using Easy Scallop, measure off increments of the size chosen in step 3, and mark the curve with a lid, plate or compass. The trick is finding the right size. (*Figure 3*)

6. Mark scallops in the same manner from both corners toward the center, adjusting the middle scallop(s) as needed. The Easy Scallop tool is infinitely adjustable. If you find you have to adjust too much in the center, then go back and check your math—you probably didn't divide accurately. (Using the blue wash-out pen, spritz the line with cold water, wait until it dries and try again.) Mark the *opposite* border in the same way. (*Figure 4*)

7. Usually a quilt is rectangular. If so, you need to refigure the size of the scallops for the remaining two borders. It makes sense that, since the two remaining borders are longer than the ones just marked, you will need one or more additional scallops along that edge. Follow steps 1 through 6 again. If the quilt is rectangular, the size of the scallop for the longer sides can be slightly different than the scallop size for the top and bottom of the quilt. As long as the scallop size stays within an inch (2.5cm) more or less of the first scallop size, it will look fine. The scallop sizes for the top and bottom of the quilt do *not* need to be the same as for the sides of the quilt, but they do need to be similar.

8. Do *not* cut on the marked line. This line is merely a *placement guide* for the binding. If you cut on the marked line, the quilt will have a bias edge, which would stretch, fray and distort. Leaving the extra fabric around the scallop ensures the edge is stable for sewing.

9. When the quilting is completed, baste on that marked line to prevent the layers from shifting when the binding is sewn on. You can hand baste or machine baste (use the longest stitch length) with a walking foot.

BINDING A SCALLOPED OR CURVED EDGE

1. Do not cut on the marked line! Quilt; then before binding, hand-baste along the marked line to keep the layers from shifting when the binding is attached. A bias binding is a must for binding curved edges. Cut a 1¼" (3.7cm) single bias binding.

2. With the raw edges of the binding aligned with the marked line on your quilt, begin sewing a ¼" (6mm) seam. Stitch to the base of the V, and stop with the needle down. Lift the presser foot.

3. Pivot the quilt and binding around the needle. Put the presser foot down and begin stitching out of the V, taking care not to stitch any pleats into the binding. *(Figure 1)*

4. Continue around the quilt in this manner, easing the binding around the curves and pivoting at the inside of the V.

5. Trim the seam allowance an even ¼" (6mm), turn the binding to the back side and stitch down by hand with matching thread, covering the stitching line. At the V, the binding will just fold over upon itself, making a little pleat.

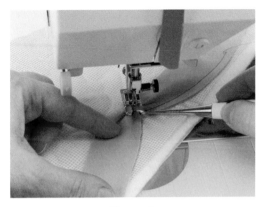

FIGURE 1

QUILT LABELS

Your quilts are your legacy—sign them! A label should include the following:

• Names of quilt recipient and quilt maker

• Date of completion/presentation

• Where the quilt was made

• Special occasion or story

You can purchase fabric labels or create your own. Sew or appliqué the label to the quilt either before or after the quilt is completed.

Tip: If you've pulled your binding too tightly on a curved edge and it causes the scallop to "cup," flatten the edge with a light steam pressing.

CURVED EDGE FINISH—"THE WAVE"

A softly curved edge with rounded corners is perfect for a small quilt or baby quilt. It also will look quite lush and fancy on a bed quilt. Of all the curved edge finishes, you will find this one the easiest to bind, as there are no V's to pivot around.

To mark a curvy (wavy) edge you must choose an *uneven* number of scallops and use a *flattened* curve.

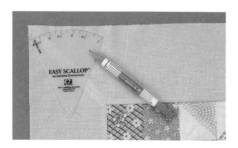

FIGURE 1

FIGURE 2

FIGURE 3

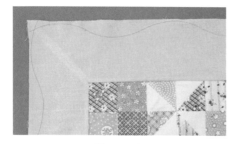

FIGURE 4

1. Measure the quilt from edge to edge.

2. Decide on the number of scallops (curves). Count both the inner and outer curves and remember to choose an uneven number.

3. Divide the length of the quilt by the number of scallops (curves). Round to the nearest ¼" (6mm). Set the Easy Scallop tool to that measurement (or, if not using the tool, refer to step 5 of *Scalloped Edge with Rounded Corners*).

4. Begin marking a full scallop at the edge of the quilt, keeping the same amount of indent on both sides of the tool. (*Figure 1*)

5. Reverse the tool and mark an upside down curve. Check to make sure the indent is the same. (*Figure 2*)

6. Repeat steps 4 and 5 at the opposite corner, working toward the center. Adjust the middle scallop (curve) as needed. Mark the opposite side the same way. (*Figure 3*)

7. Measure, divide the length by the number of scallops (an uneven number) and mark the remaining two sides. You will have a softly rounded corner automatically marked. (*Figure 4*)

8. Baste by hand (or by using the walking foot on the machine) along the marked line.

9. Bind with single bias binding cut 1¼" (3.2cm). Ease the binding around the inside and outside curves. Refer to *Binding a Scalloped or Curved Edge*.

EASY ANGLE TOOL

Easy Angle allows you to cut triangles from the same size strip as for squares. You need only to add a ½" (13mm) seam allowance when using Easy Angle, instead of the ⅞" (22mm) added when not using the tool.

To use the tool most efficiently, layer the fabric strips you are cutting for your triangles right sides together and then cut with Easy Angle. Now they are ready to be chain sewn.

Before making the first cut, trim off the selvages. Then align the small, narrow flat edge of the tool at the top of the strip matching a line on the tool with the bottom edge of the strip. Cut on the diagonal edge. (*Figure 1*)

To make the second cut, rotate the tool so the flat edge is aligned at the bottom of the strip and a line on the tool is aligned with the top of the strip. Cut again. (*Figure 2*)

Continue in this manner down the strip. Chain sew the triangles on the longest edge. Press toward the darkest fabric and trim the dog ears.

COMPANION ANGLE TOOL

Companion Angle allows you to cut quarter-square triangles with the longest edge on the straight-of-grain. A common use for this type of triangle is the goose in Flying Geese.

To cut with Companion Angle, align the top flat point of the tool with the top edge of the strip. A line on the tool should align with the bottom of the strip. Cut on both sides of the tool. (*Figure 3*)

For the next cut, rotate the tool so the point of the tool is at the bottom of the strip and a line on the tool is aligned with the top of the strip. Cut again. (*Figure 4*)

Continue in this manner down the strip of fabric.

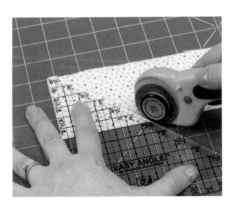

FIGURE 1

FIGURE 3

FIGURE 2

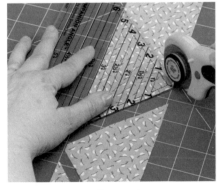

FIGURE 4

103

FREEZER-PAPER APPLIQUÉ

1. Trace the shapes on the dull side of the freezer paper, reversing the image first if necessary. (You can reuse the freezer paper several times.)

2. Cut out the shapes on the marked line. Iron the shapes to the wrong side of the fabrics chosen for the appliqué, leaving at least ¾" (20mm) between the shapes.

3. Cut out the shapes, adding a scant ¼" (6mm) seam allowance. Clip any inside curves.

4. With equal parts liquid starch and water mixture or spray starch and a cotton swab or child's paintbrush, wet the seam allowance of the appliqué piece. Using the tip of the iron, press the seam allowance over the edge of the freezer paper. Once the edge is well pressed, remove the freezer paper and iron from the right side.

5. Baste in place on the background square either with needle and thread or with basting glue.

6. Appliqué down by hand or machine zigzag with matching or invisible thread.

FUSIBLE APPLIQUÉ

1. Trace the reversed pattern on the paper side of the fusible web. Leave a bit of space between each appliqué pattern.

2. Cut out the pattern, leaving a small excess of paper around the appliqué. For a softer appliqué, cut out the center of the appliqué shape, leaving at least a ¼" (6mm) margin inside the shape. Iron to the wrong side of the fabrics chosen for the appliqué, following the manufacturer's instructions for fusing.

3. Cut out the shape on the marked line and then peel off the paper backing. Position the appliqué shape in place on the background fabric and fuse in place, following the manufacturer's directions.

4. By machine or hand, buttonhole stitch around the shapes with contrasting, matching or invisible thread.

Tip: If you iron two pieces of freezer paper together (dull side to shiny side), you'll have a much firmer template to iron the fabric around.

BORDERS

We often make adding borders to a quilt more difficult than it needs to be. Simply cut the strips designated for the borders and piece them as needed. Some people prefer to piece the borders on the diagonal, but the print can also be matched with a straight seam. Choose which method works best for your project.

Place the border strips on top of the quilt to measure the length or width of the quilt through the middle. Always measure with two border strips together so the borders are guaranteed to be the same length. Crease the border strips at the proper length, but cut an extra inch longer for leeway. Pin the borders to the quilt and sew.

MITERED CORNERS FOR BORDERS

Measure and cut borders the width (or length) of the quilt plus border width times two, plus several more inches for insurance. Sew all four borders to the quilt top, centering the borders and stitching only to ¼" (6mm) from the corners. Stop and backstitch. Press the seam allowances toward the quilt.

Fold the quilt on the diagonal, right sides together, matching raw edges and having the borders extending outward.

Lay the Companion Angle (or a ruler) on your quilt with the longest edge on the diagonal fold, and the side of the tool aligned with the raw edges of the borders. Draw a line from the diagonal fold to the edge of the borders.

Pin the borders together along this line. Stitch on the line, backstitching at the inside corner.

Check the seam on the right side. If it is properly sewn, trim the seam to ¼" (6mm) and press open.

Repeat for all four corners.

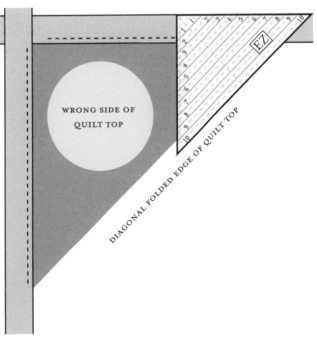

WRONG SIDE OF QUILT TOP

DIAGONAL FOLDED EDGE OF QUILT TOP

Acknowledgments

It takes a village—or at least a team of people—to put together a book. With the assistance of talented colleagues, this book was developed in record time! Many thanks to the following people and companies.

My editor Noel Rivera, Amelia Johanson and everyone else at F+W Media who transformed my ideas into a fabulous book.

My daughter, Rachel Shelburne, for her talent and expertise in drawing the illustrations and taking the step-by-step photographs.

Robert Kaufman Fabrics Co., Moda and Maywood Studios for supplying the beautiful fabrics for the projects.

EZ Quilting by Simplicity for supplying the helpful tools for the projects.

Barb Simons at Stone Ridge Quilting and Lois Sather at Country Quilting for their beautiful (and fast!) machine quilting.

Pellon for supplying batting for all the projects.

Margy Manderfeld for allowing me to teach her "Perfect Fit" binding technique.

Dedication

My unsung hero—my husband Don—deserves to have a book dedicated to him at last. I wish to acknowledge and thank him for listening, advising, supporting and encouraging me on this journey of discovery and creativity. Life is good!

ABOUT THE AUTHOR

Darlene Zimmerman is the author of ten books for F+W Media. She has been designing fabrics since 1997 and has produced two to six lines each year for Robert Kaufman Fabrics. All of the new pre-cut fabric bundles now available have inspired her to write this book of projects that use a variety of pre-cuts.

Darlene publishes approximately four patterns each year that are distributed through various outlets, including quilt shops, the Nancy's Notions website and numerous catalogs. She attends Quilt Market on behalf of Robert Kaufman and EZ Quilting by Simplicity, with whom she has a line of branded tools. She also teaches at quilt guilds and shops around the country.

In addition to quilting, she enjoys "adventure" travel and spending time with her family and grandchildren.

You can visit Darlene at her website, www.feedsacklady.com.

Resources

The tools and supplies shown in this book are from the following manufacturers. They can be found at your local quilt shop, fabric or craft store, on the web or by mail order.

American & Efird LLC
(A&E Threads)
P.O. Box 507
Mt. Holly, NC 28120
(800) 438-5868
www.amefird.com

Robert Kaufman Fabrics
129 W. 132nd St.
Los Angeles, CA 90061
(800) 877-2066
www.robertkaufman.com

EZ Quilting by Simplicity
6050 Dana Way
Antioch, TN 37013
(800) 628-9362
www.simplicity.com

Moda United Notions
13800 Hutton Dr.
Dallas, TX 75234
(800) 527-9447
www.unitednotions.com

Needlings, Inc.
Darlene Zimmerman
804 W. Main St.
Belle Plaine, MN 56011
www.feedsacklady.com

E.E. Schenck (Maywood Studio)
6000 N. Cutter Circle
Portland, OR 97217
(800) 433-0722
www.eeschenck.com

Pellon Consumer Products
150 2nd Ave. N, Suite 1400
St. Petersburg, FL 33701
(727) 388-7171
(800) 223-5275

Index

Quick Quilt Projects with Jelly Rolls, Fat Quarters, Honeybuns and Layer Cakes.
Copyright © 2013 by Darlene Zimmerman. Manufactured in China. All rights reserved.
The patterns and drawings in this book are for the personal use of the reader. By
permission of the author and publisher, they may be either hand-traced or photocopied
to make single copies, but under no circumstances may they be resold or republished.
No other part of this book may be reproduced in any form or by any electronic or
mechanical means including information storage and retrieval systems without permission in writing from the publisher, except by a reviewer who may quote brief passages in
a review. Published by KP Craft, an imprint of F+W Media, Inc., 10151 Carver Road,
Ste. 200, Cincinnati, Ohio, 45242. (800) 289-0963. First Edition.

www.fwmedia.com

17 16 15 14 13   5 4 3 2 1

DISTRIBUTED IN CANADA BY FRASER DIRECT
100 Armstrong Avenue
Georgetown, ON, Canada L7G 5S4
Tel: (905) 877-4411

DISTRIBUTED IN THE U.K. AND EUROPE BY F&W MEDIA INTERNATIONAL
Brunel House, Newton Abbot, Devon, TQ12 4PU, England
Tel: (+44) 1626 323200, Fax: (+44) 1626 323319
E-mail: enquiries@fwmedia.com

DISTRIBUTED IN AUSTRALIA BY CAPRICORN LINK
P.O. Box 704, S. Windsor NSW, 2756 Australia
Tel: (02) 4560-1600 Fax: 02 4577-5288
books@capricornlink.com

SRN: U5867
ISBN-10: 1-4402-3787-5
ISBN-13: 978-1-4402-3787-4

Edited by **Noel Rivera**
Designed by **Kelly Pace**
Illustrations by **Rachel Shelburne**
Production coordinated by **Greg Nock**
Photography by **Corrie Schaffeld with 1326 Studios**
Photo Styling by **Lauren Siedentopf with Luna Root Studio**

METRIC CONVERSION CHART

To convert	to	multiply by
Inches	Centimeters	2.54
Centimeters	Inches	0.4
Feet	Centimeters	30.5
Centimeters	Feet	0.03
Yards	Meters	0.9
Meters	Yards	1.1

BLUE-AND-WHITE CLASSIC QUILT

LAKE COUNTRY QUILT

MORE FANTASTIC QUILTING TITLES!

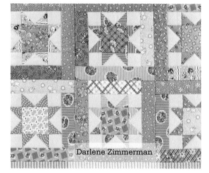

FRESH FROM THE CLOTHESLINE

Quilts and Small Projects with Vintage Appeal

by Darlene Zimmerman

Fresh from the Clothesline features twenty-two fat-quarter and fat-eighth friendly quilts and projects of all sizes in Darlene Zimmerman's signature style. Try them in different colors and combinations to make your own beautiful creations.

ISBN-13: 978-1-4402-1775-3
SRN: W0937

QUILT ESSENTIALS: QUILT FINISHES

Techniques and Embellishments for Fabulous Edges

by Darlene Zimmerman

Quilt Essentials: Quilt Finishes provides tips and techniques for creating several popular quilt edges, including flanged, pieced and scalloped, while including four projects inspired by the beauty of Oregan's Lavender Hill Farm.

ISBN-13: 978-1-4402-3637-2
SRN: U3860

QUILTING: THE COMPLETE GUIDE

by Darlene Zimmerman

Quilting: The Complete Guide lives up to its name! It covers all of the essential knowledge you need to complete any quilting project, including tools, formulas, methods, finishing techniques and quilt care. It's the perfect companion for all your quilting projects.

ISBN-13: 978-1-4402-3887-1
SRN: U8350